GARDENS

Schweiz/Suisse/Switzerland

GARDENS

Schweiz/Suisse/Switzerland

HESTER MACDONALD

52 botanical gems that inspire and astound

TABLE OF CONTENTS

Swiss Gardens Schweiz/Suisse/Switzerland

INTRODUCTION

Switzerland has, without a doubt, some of the world's most beautiful gardens, and almost all of them are open to the public at little or no cost. Certainly no country of similar size can offer such an incredible diversity of plants, from the desert cacti of the Sukkulenten Sammlung in Zurich, to the alpine beauties of the Schynige Platte, or such a huge variety of styles, types and sizes of gardens, from the huge landscape park at Elfenau in Bern, to the compact but stunning modern perennials garden at the Jardin d'Amandolier in Geneva. In the gardening world, Switzerland is a giant – just waiting to be discovered.

This book contains 52 gardens, across the country, split up by canton. There are modern gardens, traditional gardens, urban gardens, country gardens and even some alpine gardens too. I've tried to find interesting examples of all the different gardens to be found in this small and very diverse country. There are also additional chapters that dig a little deeper into some iconic plants and garden types, so you can enjoy these wonderful plants at home.

Gardens Switzerland Suisse Schweiz is for everyone interested in gardens, plants and garden visiting. Perhaps you're visiting for the first time and want some suggestions for places to visit, or maybe you're a long-time resident, or even a holder of a coveted red passport, and want to discover somewhere new in your own city. These gardens are suitable for families, and people with reduced mobility – just check the icons and the information panels for each of the gardens.

My criteria for choosing the gardens were broad – they must be open at least 10 days per year, they must be accessible by public transport, and they should have more than one season of interest.

There are lots of amazing gardens that didn't fit these criteria, of course, and this is not a comprehensive guide to every Swiss garden, but there are enough of them to visit a new one every week of the year, should you be lucky enough.

Since 2003, I've been profiling the gardens and interviewing head gardeners and garden makers on my radio show, *Dig It! on World* Radio Switzerland. This book is for all my wonderful listeners and also for those who haven't tuned in yet. When I'm not on the radio I'm a garden designer, horticulturalist, garden guide, founder of a gardening school and a garden enthusiast, and all these gardens have inspired and delighted me. I hope they inspire and delight you too.

Swiss gardens are varied, beautifully maintained, creatively inspiring and deserve to be better known both within and outside Switzerland. This book is intended to help visitors get to know them better, so pick a garden, grab your camera and get out there!

Thanks

My thanks to friends and colleagues who suggested gardens to visit, and the garden owners and directors who welcomed me. If I got anything wrong about your wonderful gardens, the fault is all mine! My thanks also to the team at Bergli Books: Richard, editor extraordinaire, who supported this project from the start; and Satu, Kali, Melanie, and Kim for making it look fantastic. My family, particularly my husband who copy-edited and re-read every single word, and my daughter who photo-edited brilliantly. Huge thanks also to the tourist boards, cities, and locals who made visiting their beautiful regions such a pleasure.

Swiss Gardens Schweiz/Suisse/Switzerland

1 CONSERVATOIRE ET JARDIN BOTANIQUE GENÈVE

With a fine historical pedigree and a connection to the most famous Swiss botanist, Augustin Pyramus de Candolle, this garden was founded in the city centre, at the Parc des Bastions. It was moved in 1904, and the new, much larger, site allowed the addition of more greenhouses, including the magnificent temperate Palm House, a winter garden and several tropical houses. The mature trees in the arboretum provide plenty of shade in summer, perfect for the lunchtime runners that lope along the paths. Rockeries, a pond, rhododendrons, a mini-zoo, an aviary and a Jules Verne-esque merry-go-round are among the other attractions.

Mit einem erlesenen historischen Stammbaum und einer Verbindung zum berühmtesten Schweizer Botaniker Augustin Pyramus de Candolle wurde dieser Garten im Genfer Stadtzentrum, im Parc des Bastions, angelegt. Er wurde 1904 an einen anderen Ort verlegt und das neue, viel grössere Gelände ermöglichte den Bau weiterer Gewächshäuser, darunter das prächtige temperierte Palmenhaus, ein Wintergarten und mehrere Tropenhäuser. Die ausgewachsenen Bäume im Arboretum spenden im Sommer viel Schatten, perfekt für Jogger, die dort in den Mittagspausen eine Runde drehen. Steingärten, ein Teich, Rhododendren, ein Mini-Zoo, eine Voliere und ein Jules Verne-ähnliches Karussell gehören zu den weiteren Attraktionen.

S'inscrivant dans une longue tradition historique et fondé par le plus connu des botanistes suisses, Augustin Pyramus de Candolle, ce jardin se situait d'abord au centre-ville, dans le Parc des Bastions. Il fut déménagé en 1904 afin de pouvoir jouir d'un espace plus grand, ce qui a permis l'ajout de serres supplémentaires, y compris la magnifique serre tempérée, le jardin d'hiver ainsi que plusieurs serres tropicales. Les grands arbres de l'arboretum offrent de larges espaces ombragés en été, parfaits pour les personnes qui profitent de l'heure du déjeuner pour courir. Des rocailles, un étang, des rhododrons, un petit parc aux animaux, une volière et un carrousel digne des romans de Jules Verne vous y attendent, parmi d'autres attractions encore.

ADDRESS: Chemin de l'Impératrice 1, 1292 Chambésy-Genève

TRANSPORT: Jardin Botanique, bus 1, 11, 25, 28, train Genève-Sécheron

VISITOR INFORMATION: Opening hours in winter 8–17, summer 8–19:30. Glasshouses have shorter opening hours than the park

HIGHLIGHTS: A popular park with tourists, families and lunchtime runners, it has something to offer everyone – a turn on the merry-go-round, alpine rockeries and large lawns on which to relax and watch the world go by.

2 JARDIN DE LA PAIX

Small but perfectly formed, this quiet park has all the elements of a well-balanced urban park. There is a small greenhouse of cacti and tender tropical plants; there are mirror pools surrounded by decking, perfect for sitting or lying on to better watch the fish; and there is a glorious pergola draped with grapevines. The crowning glory of this park is the impeccable planting, arranged chromatically from the white and green grasses by the pergola, through the bright yellows to reds, oranges, pinks and on to the blues and purples at the entrance: a paint palette in plants with roses, grasses, perennials and shrubs.

Klein, aber perfekt gestaltet – dieser ruhige Park vereint alle Elemente eines ausgewogenen Stadtparks. Da gibt es ein kleines Gewächshaus mit Kakteen und zarten tropischen Pflanzen, es gibt ein von Holzdeck eingerahmtes Spiegelbecken, an dem man perfekt sitzen oder liegen kann, um die Fische zu beobachten. Ausserdem gibt es eine herrliche, mit Weinreben überwachsene Pergola. Die Krönung dieses Parks ist die makellose Bepflanzung, die chromatisch von weissen und grünen Gräsern bei der Pergola über das leuchtende Gelb zu Rot-, Orange- und Rosatönen bis hin zu Blau und Lila am Eingang angeordnet ist: eine Pflanzenfarbpalette mit Rosen, Gräsern, Stauden und Sträuchern.

Ce petit parc au calme possède tous les éléments nécessaires à l'équilibre d'un parc urbain. Il est agrémenté d'une petite serre remplie de cactus et de délicates plantes tropicales ainsi que de bassins à effet miroir entourés de terrasses en bois, idéales pour y observer tranquillement les poissons – le tout décoré d'une splendide pergola habillée de vignes. La touche finale de ce parc est l'agencement impeccable des plantes de manière chromatique : près de la pergola, la pelouse est vêtue de blanc et de vert, puis, les couleurs se réchauffent et se transforment en des teintes éclatantes de jaune, de rouge, d'orange et de rose, jusqu'à des nuances plus froides de bleu et de violet près de l'entrée. Une véritable palette de peinture formée de roses, d'herbes, de plantes vivaces et d'arbrisseaux.

ADDRESS: Rue de l'Industrie, Rue Moillebeau, Genève 1209

TRANSPORT: Moillebeau bus 3, NE or Trembley 3, 22, NE

VISITOR INFORMATION: Opening hours in winter 7:30–17, summer 7–19

HIGHLIGHTS: The garden is dedicated to the memory of Sergio Vieira de Mello and his team who died in Iraq working for the UN.

Swiss Gardens Schweiz/Suisse/Switzerland

3 LE JARDIN D'AMANDOLIER

Creating a modern garden in the heart of this traditional neighbourhood of Geneva is a brave thing to do, but the garden here is a roaring success, blending materials, plants and buildings seamlessly – and all without upsetting the *grandes dames* of the large private houses nearby. The garden is the result of an international competition, won by the design agency TER, and the entire development was managed by SPG-RYTZ. The garden is just as lovely from the offices above as for the passers-by on foot or on the tram. Head around the green wall and you'll find a remarkable arrangement of Corten steel misting devices and benches, as well as soft, inviting plantings, including grasses and splashes of perennial colour.

Einen modernen Garten im Herzen dieses traditionellen Stadtteils von Genf zu kreieren, erfordert Mut. Aber der Garten ist ein voller Erfolg, weil er Materialien, Pflanzen und Gebäude miteinander verbindet – und das, ohne die *Grandes Dames* in den umliegenden grossen Privatresidenzen zu stören. Der Garten ist das Resultat eines internationalen Wettbewerbs, den die Designagentur TER gewonnen hat. Die Entwicklung wurde von SPG-RYTZ organisiert. Von oben aus den Büros gesehen ist der Garten genauso hübsch wie für die Passanten, die hier zu Fuss oder in der Strassenbahn vorbeikommen. Geht man um die grüne Wand herum, trifft man auf eine bemerkenswerte Anordnung von Wasserzerstäubern und Sitzgelegenheiten aus Cortenstahl sowie auf einladende Bepflanzungen, darunter Gräser und farbige Mehrjährige.

Créer un jardin moderne au sein du quartier traditionnel de Genève est une chose audacieuse à faire, mais le défi a été relevé avec brio, le jardin connaissant un succès fou avec son mélange harmonieux de matériaux, de plantes et d'immeubles – le tout sans contrarier les grandes dames des maisons particulières se trouvant juste à côté. Fruit d'un concours international gagné par l'agence TER, le projet fut réalisé par Asset Development du groupe SPG-RYTZ. Ce jardin est tout aussi charmant vu du haut des bureaux que pour les passants qui le longent à pied ou en tram. Approchez-vous du mur végétal pour y trouver un agencement remarquable de brumisateurs et de bancs en acier Corten ainsi que des plantes attrayantes à l'aspect doux, de la pelouse et des touches de couleurs posées çà et là grâce aux jolies plantes vivaces.

ADDRESS: Route de Chêne 30, 1208 Genève

TRANSPORT: Amandolier tram 12, buses 21 nd NK

VISITOR INFORMATION: Open at all hours, every day

HIGHLIGHTS: This is a private garden, belonging to the offices above, the public are invited in, but please behave accordingly.

PERENNIALLY SWISS

Perennials are plants that live for more than two years, as opposed to the plants that we describe as "annuals" that develop, flower and die in one year. Trees and shrubs, of course, live for more than two years, but the plants that most people recognise as perennials are "herbaceous perennials" – that is to say, they are non-woody plants that die back to the ground in autumn; the roots survive the winter underground, and the plant grows again in the spring.

In most regions of Switzerland, with hard winters and long, gentle autumns, perennials are a perfect partner for bringing lots of colour and interest to borders and containers from early spring right up to the first snow, and as a result, the Swiss interest in using perennials pre-dates the current fashion for them by several decades. The Swiss breeder, Frikart, was founded in Stäfa in 1908, and their enduringly popular aster, *Aster x frikartii*, *"Wunder von Stäfa"* still sells well today, despite being nearly 100 years old.

The European perennial movement is one that promotes naturalistic planting, with plants ecologically adapted for their situation, in colonies and groups that might be found together. It is suitable for urban gardens and parks, where the communes need to reduce costs and ecological impact, as well as for home gardens with a bit less space. You can see some great examples of research on plant mixes at the ZHAW garden (page 115) in Wädenswil, a living laboratory for low-care plant combinations. You can choose from one of four blends, such as "Indian Sunset", which is dominated by grasses with lots of rich oranges and yellows, suitable for a sunny situation, and is intended to bring maintenance down to an incredible 8 minutes per year, per square metre. Or perhaps you might prefer the blues and purples of "Sommerwind", and the inclusion of the lovely *Aster x frikartii "Wunder von Stäfa"* for a really Swiss perennials planting.

Amazingly, perennials planting can also be found in historic formal gardens, too. The Wenkenpark in Riehen (page 77) has a fabulous modern planting, in the French formal garden, which works very well with the historic Wenkenhof as a backdrop.

Swiss Gardens Schweiz/Suisse/Switzerland

4 ARBORETUM DU VALLON DE L'AUBONNE

In the secluded Aubonne Valley, you will find a perfect example of an arboretum. Several thousand different trees, all well-labelled, are scattered throughout the valley. Grouped together in botanical families, there are collections of cedars, oaks, and birch as well as various conifers. You can also enjoy cherry, apple and pear orchards as well as a collection of wild roses. A well-planned arboretum like this can provide hours of study for the specialist, or just a gentle stroll for a family, far from any roads, among beautiful trees and a stunning setting.

Im abgelegenen Aubonnetal trifft man auf ein perfektes Beispiel für ein Arboretum. Mehrere tausend unterschiedliche, gut gekennzeichnete Baumarten stehen hier im ganzen Tal verstreut. In botanischen Familien gruppiert gibt es Ansammlungen von Zedern, Eichen und Birken sowie verschiedenen Nadelbäumen. Auch an Kirsch-, Apfel- und Birnenhainen sowie einer Ansammlung von Wildrosen kann man sich erfreuen. Ein gut geplantes Arboretum wie dieses ermöglicht dem Spezialisten ein stundenlanges Studium oder bietet einer Familie ganz einfach die Möglichkeit zu einem gemütlichen Spaziergang zwischen schönen Bäumen und in einer atemberaubenden Umgebung fernab von Strassen.

Dans le vallon isolé de l'Aubonne, vous trouverez l'exemple parfait d'un arboretum. Plusieurs milliers d'arbres différents, tous décorés d'une étiquette, sont éparpillés dans l'ensemble de la petite vallée. Réunis par famille botanique, vous irez à la rencontre de cèdres, de chênes et de bouleaux ainsi que de divers conifères. Vous attendent également des vergers de cerisiers, de pommiers et de poiriers, agrémentés d'une collection de roses sauvages. Un arboretum bien planifié comme celui-ci peut occuper un spécialiste durant des heures entières, mais il se prête tout aussi bien à une petite promenade en famille, loin de la circulation, vous plongeant dans un cadre arboré tout à fait exceptionnel.

ADDRESS: Chemin de Plan 92, 1170 Aubonne

TRANSPORT: Montherod-Battoir, plus 1.7km walk

VISITOR INFORMATION: Every day, all year

HIGHLIGHTS: The Arboretum has lots of special events, like the Japanese cherry blossom festival, as well as regular guided tours from spring to autumn. See website for details.

Swiss Gardens Schweiz/Suisse/Switzerland

5 AU DIABLE VERT

Would you prefer a hobbit garden or a miniature Monet's Giverny? How about a modern rose garden where the roses are grouped by family, with "Princess Grace" next to the "Jubilé Prince de Monaco" for company? Or a chessboard garden? And all of it encased with extraordinary views in every direction? This private garden, open to the public, is a reflection of the owners' decades of experience with plants and their interests in alternative methods of growing and healing. Take off your shoes, walk the paths, sit on the grass and admire the extraordinarily healthy plants. Sculptures, art and curiosities complete the experience.

Lieber einen Hobbit-Garten oder eine Miniatur von Monets Giverny? Wie wäre es mit einem modernen Rosengarten, in dem die Rosen nach Familien geordnet sind, wie z.B. ‹Princess Grace› in Gesellschaft von ‹Jubilé Prince de Monaco›? Oder ein Schachbrettgarten? Und das alles umrahmt von aussergewöhnlichen Ausblicken in alle Richtungen? Dieser öffentlich zugängliche Privatgarten spiegelt die jahrzehntelange Erfahrung der Besitzer mit Pflanzen und ihr Interesse an alternativen Anbau- und Heilmethoden wider. Ziehen Sie Ihre Schuhe aus, folgen Sie dem Pfad, setzen Sie sich auf das Gras und bewundern Sie die äusserst gesunden Pflanzen. Skulpturen, Kunst und Kuriositäten runden das Erlebnis ab.

Que préféreriez-vous : un jardin de hobbit ou une miniature du jardin de Monet à Giverny ? Et pourquoi pas un jardin moderne rempli de roses présentées par famille, avec « Princess Grace » en compagnie de « Jubilé Prince de Monaco » ? Ou encore un jardin décoré d'un échiquier ? Et tout cela entouré de superbes paysages de toute part ? Ce jardin privé ouvert au public est le reflet de la grande expérience botanique de ses propriétaires et de l'intérêt qu'ils accordent aux méthodes alternatives pour faire pousser les plantes et soigner avec ces dernières. Ôtez vos chaussures, empruntez les divers chemins, asseyez-vous dans l'herbe et admirez ces plantes incroyablement saines. Des sculptures, des œuvres d'art ainsi que d'autres curiosités complètent votre petite aventure.

ADDRESS: Route de Magny 45, 1880 Bex

TRANSPORT: Bex train

VISITOR INFORMATION: Opening hours Mon–Fri 10–12, 14–18, Saturday 10–17, Sunday closed. Costs 5 CHF for adults

HIGHLIGHTS: A truly remarkable, varied garden with a Hobbit garden, a miniature Giverny and a modern rose garden, all cared for under biodynamic principles

6 CHÂTEAU DE PRANGINS

Although this garden is at its most splendid and productive in the summer months, I prefer it in late winter. With the frost melting on the cabbages, cardoons blanching in their sacks, and the first brave shoots appearing on the espaliered fruit trees, it is a magical place. In the pale winter light and with a quiet half hour, you can imagine yourself back nearly three centuries to the time of the first Baron Guiguer, when small boys scratched for weeds between the rows. The garden was reconstructed and replanted in 1998, and is full of heritage varieties saved from extinction, beautifully arranged and organically grown.

Obwohl dieser Garten in den Sommermonaten am prächtigsten und produktivsten ist, bevorzuge ich ihn im Spätwinter. Mit schmelzendem Frost auf den Kohlköpfen, den in ihren Säcken verbleichenden Kardonen und den ersten mutigen auf den Spalierobstbäumen erscheinenden Trieben ist es ein magischer Ort. Im blassen Winterlicht und einer ruhigen halben Stunde kann man sich zurückversetzen lassen in die Zeit des ersten Barons Guiguer vor fast drei Jahrhunderten, als kleine Jungen zwischen den Reihen Unkraut zupften. Der Garten wurde 1998 rekonstruiert und wiederbepflanzt und ist voller alter Varianten, die vor dem Aussterben gerettet wurden, schön angelegt und organisch gewachsen.

Bien que ce jardin connaisse ses plus beaux jours lors des mois d'été, je le préfère à la fin de l'hiver. C'est un endroit magique où le givre se forme sur les choux tandis que les cardons blanchissent dans leurs sacs et les premières pousses apparaissent sur les arbres fruitiers formés en espalier. En l'espace d'une demiheure, au calme et sous la lumière pâle de l'hiver, vous pouvez vous imaginer trois siècles en arrière au temps du premier baron Guiguer, où des garçons désherbaient entre les rangées de plantes. Le jardin fut reconstruit et replanté en 1998 et est à présent rempli d'anciennes variétés sauvées de l'extinction, joliment présentées et cultivées biologiquement.

ADDRESS: Avenue Général Guiguer 3, 1197 Prangins

TRANSPORT: Bus 805, stop Prangins Musée National

VISITOR INFORMATION: Opening hours Tuesday-Sunday 10–17, closed public holidays. There is no fee to visit the garden.

HIGHLIGHTS: Experience history brought to life in the walled vegetable garden with heritage varieties of fruit, herbs, vegetables and other useful plants

7 JARDIN DES IRIS

The iris gardens at the Château de Vullierens provide an eagerly-awaited spectacle for local garden fans and casual visitors alike. The gardens are centred around a large iris collection, started in 1950 by the mother of the current owner. These provide several weeks of colour in late spring and again in autumn, and the collection has been augmented by the introduction of several new gardens, with the intention of broadening the appeal – and lengthening the flowering season for visitors. There are now also hundreds of spring-flowering bulbs, a romantic waterside garden, a mysterious dell, a rose garden and some lovely rhododendrons.

Die Irisgärten des Château de Vullierens bieten ein alljährlich herbeigesehntes Spektakel für die Gartenfreunde vor Ort sowie Gelegenheitsgäste. Im Mittelpunkt des Gartens trifft man auf eine grosse Iris-Sammlung, die 1950 von der Mutter des jetzigen Besitzers angelegt wurde. Die Blumen sorgen im späten Frühjahr und dann wieder im Herbst für mehrere Wochen voller Farbenpracht. Diese Sammlung wurde durch die Einführung mehrerer neuer Gärten ergänzt, um die Attraktivität des Gartens zu erhöhen sowie die Blütezeit für die Besucher zu verlängern. Heute gibt es dort auch Hunderte von im Frühling blühenden Zwiebelgewächsen, einen romantischen Ufergarten, eine mysteriöse Mulde, einen Rosengarten und einige schöne Rhododendren.

Au château de Vullierens, les jardins des iris offrent un spectacle très attendu par les amoureux espaces verts du coin tout comme par les visiteurs occasionnels. Les jardins, se trouvant au centre, sont entourés d'une grande collection d'iris dont la mère du propriétaire actuel a été l'initiatrice en 1950. Ils créent une véritable mosaïque de couleurs durant plusieurs semaines, à la fin du printemps et à nouveau en automne. Cette collection a été agrandie en introduisant plusieurs nouveaux jardins afin de rendre le tout plus attrayant et de rallonger la période de floraison pour le plaisir les visiteurs. À présent, on y trouve aussi des centaines de bulbes de printemps, un jardin romantique au bord de l'eau, un vallon mystérieux, un jardin de roses et quelques charmants rhododendrons.

ADDRESS: Les Jardins du Château de Vullierens, 1115 Vullierens

TRANSPORT: Vullierens Village bus 730, 731, 791

VISITOR INFORMATION: Costs 15 CHF for adults and children 12–15, 5 CHF. Under 12's free. Opens mid-April to end-May every day 9–18h. Also 13:30–18 Tuesday–Sunday June–July.

HIGHLIGHTS: The garden is only open when the irises and other flowers are at their best. Don't miss it!

8 JARDIN D'EXPOSITION

Nurseries have been making show gardens for many years, but rarely have I found one that enchanted and engaged me as much as this one. The nursery was founded in 1964 by the grandfather of the current owners, and many of the recent additions – like the perennial garden and the inspiration garden – are thanks to them. It's a place to wander round, notebook in hand, if you've a new tree or shrub to plant, or just enjoy the experience and leave with lots of great photos.

Baumschulen legen seit vielen Jahren Schaugärten an, aber selten habe ich einen gesehen, der mich so sehr verzaubert und angesprochen hat wie dieser. Die Baumschule wurde 1964 vom Grossvater der heutigen Besitzer gegründet, und viele der jüngsten Ergänzungen – wie der Staudengarten und der Inspirationsgarten – haben wir ihnen zu verdanken. Es ist ein Ort, an dem man mit einem Notizbuch in der Hand herumspazieren kann, wenn man einen neuen Baum oder Strauch pflanzen möchte und Inspiration sucht – oder man geniesst einfach nur die Erfahrung und kehrt mit vielen grossartigen Fotos heim.

Cela fait de nombreuses années que les pépinières créent des jardins d'exposition, mais j'en ai rarement vu un qui m'enchante et m'attire à ce point. La pépinière fut fondée en 1964 par le grand-père des propriétaires actuels, grâce auxquels un grand nombre de récents ajouts sont venus l'agrémenter – comme le jardin des plantes vivaces et le jardin d'inspiration. C'est un endroit dans lequel il est agréable de se promener, un cahier sous la main, où vous pouvez planter un nouvel arbre ou un arbrisseau, ou encore tout simplement profiter de votre visite et repartir avec plein de superbes photos.

ADDRESS: Ch. de Camarès 1, 1032 Vernand-sur-Lausanne

TRANSPORT: Vernand-Camarès train RLEB

VISITOR INFORMATION: Office hours Mon–Fri 7:30–12, 13:15–17:30, Saturday 7:30–12. To find the garden, use the address Chemin des Mésanges, 1032 Romanel-sur-Lausanne. They are at the end of the road!

HIGHLIGHTS: The perennial garden is superb in summer and the autumn leaf colour is magical

CONIFERS

Conifers are remarkable plants. They first appeared 300 million years ago, in the Permian period, long before the dinosaurs, and although their dominance was surpassed by the flowering plants, we have many species left to us today.

Although they are outnumbered and outcompeted by flowering plants, they are particularly well adapted for living in conditions inhospitable to other plants, from tropical to almost Arctic. They make excellent pioneers, thriving on soils that have low fertility, or are badly drained, or are regularly attacked by fire. They are ideal for areas with cold snowy winters, as their naturally conical shape allows snow to slide off easily. Many of them grow to great sizes, such as the huge Sequioa in Thun, at 38m tall and with a circumference of 8.8m. Many of them can also reach a great age. The oldest tree in Switzerland is probably a yew, a conifer, and is estimated to be about 1500 years, found in the Maljon forest, in Crémines in the Canton of Bern. This is a young whipper-snapper in comparison to the Llangernyw yew in Wales estimated to be at least 4000 years old, planted in the Bronze Age.

Because conifers can live so long, they often have interesting stories attached to them. The Lebanon Cedar in the Parc Beaulieu in Geneva was one of the first cedars planted in the city. The French botanist Bernard de Jussieu had collected seeds in England from trees planted there, and then germinated the seeds in Paris at the Jardin des Plantes. Legend says that he transported some of these precious seedlings in his hat and, in 1735, gave a few of these to the writer and patron, François de Sellon, who had his house in what became the Parc de Beaulieu. The cedar today is about 27m tall with sturdy low-hanging branches skimming the ground, perfect for playing in and around.

Cedars are well represented in Geneva, with 3800 of them out of 40,000 listed trees in the city. There is even a walk that you can take, titled "From Cedar to Cedar" planned by the Tourist Office of Geneva, taking in 22 of the largest, oldest or most curious of these trees in Geneva.

9 EVOLOGIA

The traditional garden of "rooms" has never been so exciting as here in the heart of the Val-de-Ruz. Each garden has a distinct flavour: some are temporary, and some, like the Bee Garden or the Hedge Garden, are permanent. The site was previously a school of agriculture, and remains dedicated to educating visitors about the agricultural and cultural offerings of the landscape around the canton. It's all done with a great sense of creativity and fun, as well as providing education and information about ecology, farming and local flora.

Noch nie war der traditionelle Garten mit seinen ‹Räumen› so spannend wie hier im Herzen des Val-de-Ruz. Jeder Garten hat seine typischen Eigenheiten: Einige sind temporär, andere, wie der Bienengarten oder der Heckengarten, sind permanent. Das Gelände der ehemaligen Landwirtschaftsschule ist nach wie vor der Information seiner Besucher über das landwirtschaftliche und kulturelle Angebot in der Landschaft des Kantons gewidmet. Dies wird mit viel Kreativität und Spassfaktor dargeboten, wobei Informationen zu Ökologie, Landwirtschaft und örtlicher Flora vermittelt werden.

Le concept traditionnel d'un jardin structuré en plusieurs espaces différents n'a jamais été aussi passionnant qu'à cet endroit, au cœur du Val-de-Ruz. Chaque jardin possède un caractère propre – certains sont temporaires, et d'autres, comme l'espace abeilles ou le jardin des haies, sont permanents. Auparavant, le site était une école d'agriculture ; de nos jours, il est consacré à l'instruction de ses visiteurs, leur offrant des informations sur le patrimoine agricole et culturel du canton. Le tout est réalisé avec beaucoup de créativité, rendant l'expérience très divertissante, ainsi qu'avec un côté éducatif et informatif en matière d'écologie, d'agriculture et de flore locale.

ADDRESS: Route de l'Aurore 6, 2053 Cernier

TRANSPORT: Evologia, bus 422

VISITOR INFORMATION: The gardens are free to visit all day, every day, but not every garden is open all winter.

HIGHLIGHTS: Current highlights include the Bee Garden, Gulliver and the well-named Extraordinary Gardens.

Swiss Gardens Schweiz/Suisse/Switzerland

10 JARDIN BOTANIQUE NEUCHÂTEL

At only 20 years young, Neuchâtel is the youngest of the Swiss botanical gardens. Perched above the city, it's a steep walk or an easy bus ride from the station, but it's a world away from the noise and traffic in town. The site is in the valley of the Ermitage, and provides a natural sound barrier from the town. The design of the garden makes good use of the hillsides, with a woodland walk on one side and the alpine and rockery beds on the other. The orchard and valley walk provide plenty of space to run around, and the excellent learning garden is fun and interactive, whatever your level of interest in plants.

Mit seinen 20 Jahren ist der Botanische Garten in Neuenburg der jüngste in der Schweiz. Zu seinem Standort am Berg oberhalb der Stadt ist es ein steiler Spaziergang oder eine bequeme Busfahrt vom Bahnhof aus. Der Garten liegt schön weit weg vom Lärm und Verkehr der Stadt, in der Talmulde der Ermitage, die eine natürliche Schallmauer zur Stadt darstellt. Die Gartengestaltung macht sich die Hanglage zunutze: mit einem Waldpfad auf der einen Seite sowie alpinen und Steingartenbeeten auf der anderen. Im Obstgarten und entlang dem Talpfad gibt es viel Platz zum Herumlaufen, und der grossartige Lehrgarten ist sowohl lustig als auch interaktiv, er bietet für jedes Mass an Interesse an Pflanzen das Richtige.

À tout juste 20 ans, Neuchâtel est le jardin botanique le plus jeune de Suisse. Surplombant la ville, on le rejoint soit en empruntant un sentier escarpé, soit – alternative plus commode – en prenant le bus. Une fois arrivé, vous serez plongé dans un monde loin de tout bruit, éloigné du trafic citadin : se trouvant dans le vallon de l'Ermitage, ce dernier offre au site un véritable mur anti-bruit naturel. La forme du jardin est parfaitement adaptée aux flancs de coteau, présentant, d'un côté, un sentier menant vers la forêt, et de l'autre, une rocaille de plantes alpines. Grâce au verger et au chemin donnant sur la vallée, il y a plus qu'assez d'espace pour se dégourdir les jambes, et les parcours pédagogiques sont à la fois amusants et interactifs – ne les manquez pas !

ADDRESS: Chemin du Pertuis-du-Sault 58, 2000 Neuchâtel

TRANSPORT: Bus 106, 209 Ermitage, or Funiculaire Ecluse Plan

VISITOR INFORMATION: Opening hours April–October 10–18, November–March 12–16. Free to visit.

HIGHLIGHTS: A well-planned, fun and educational garden in the heart of a beautiful natural valley

11 JARDIN DU PEYROU

Dominated by the pair of Sphinxes that guard the entrance to the garden, this eighteenth century French formal garden is a magical find for a visitor. With the gently trickling fountain, clipped yew topiary, boxwood parterres and exuberant seasonal planting, you can easily imagine yourself at Versailles. There are plenty of benches to perch on and wonder what the garden must have been like when it stretched all the way to the lake – a vista now rudely interrupted by development. If you visit on a day when the restaurant is closed, you'll have the garden almost to yourself, apart from the blackbirds in the magnolia tree.

Dominiert von dem Sphinxenpaar, das den Eingang zum Garten bewacht, ist dieser Barockgarten aus dem 18. Jahrhundert ein magischer Fund für Besucher. Mit dem sanft plätschernden Springbrunnen, der in Formschnitt gestutzten Eibe, den Buchsbaum-Parterres und der üppigen saisonalen Bepflanzung wähnt man sich fast in Versailles. Es gibt viele Bänke zum Sitzen und man fragt sich, wie der Garten wohl gewesen sein mag, als er sich bis zum See erstreckte – eine Aussicht, die jetzt abrupt von Gebäuden unterbrochen wird. Besucht man den Garten an einem Tag, an dem das Restaurant geschlossen ist, hat man den Garten fast für sich allein, wenn man mal von den Amseln im Magnolienbaum absieht.

Ce jardin classique de style français du dix-huitième siècle, dont l'entrée est bravement gardée par un couple de sphinx, est une trouvaille tout à fait magique pour ses visiteurs. Avec sa fontaine au murmure cristallin, ses ifs taillés en topiaire, son parterre en buis et ses plantes saisonnières exubérantes, vous pouvez facilement vous imaginer à Versailles. Il y a un grand nombre de bancs sur lesquels vous asseoir pour profiter d'une pause durant laquelle vous pouvez vous imaginer ce à quoi ressemblait le jardin lorsqu'il s'étendait jusqu'au lac – une vue qui, à présent et au nom du développement, n'est plus. Si vous venez un jour où le restaurant est fermé, vous aurez probablement la chance d'être pratiquement seul, sans compter bien sûr la compagnie des merles perchés dans le magnolia.

ADDRESS: Avenue DuPeyrou 1, CH-2000 Neuchâtel (NB this gives an odd result on google maps, but it is the correct address)

TRANSPORT: Jardin Anglais bus 101. 121

VISITOR INFORMATION: The garden is free to visit any time, every day of the year. Access at the restaurant end of the garden may be more limited in summer.

HIGHLIGHTS: Sumptuous seasonal bedding and elegant evergreen topiary make this small garden a must-see gem in Neuchâtel.

COTTAGE GARDENS SWISS STYLE

Wherever I go, I'm always peeking into people's gardens, to see what they're growing, and how. I've even been known to go and knock on the door of a house to ask about a particular plant, much to the embarrassment of my children. What makes my heart really sing though, here in Switzerland, are the small but perfectly-formed cottage gardens seen in the countryside, the *Bauerngärten*.

Here every bit of space is efficiently used, in the vertical plane as well as the horizontal, with fruit trees grown on the warmest walls for the best ripening, providing fruit for eating, cooking, drying, and maybe even cider or *eau de vie* if there are enough. A lot of effort goes into efficiently working the soil here, the neat rows of carefully-hoed vegetables usually have a second crop already seeded and waiting to take over when the first crop is picked. The people that plan and manage these gardens must have ferociously detailed notebooks to keep track of what grew where and when, so as not to exhaust the soil.

For me, it's the ideal combination of the beautiful and the useful, as the gardens are often edged with boxwood, or another low-growing evergreen to give symmetry and structure. Paths leading from the house are edged with stone or brick, and allow the garden-owners easy access even in the height of summer when the produce escapes from the beds onto the path. Flowers are grown alongside the vegetables, as companion planting for the vegetables to encourage beneficial insects and to deter pests. They are also used to dress the house or the church and often for making home remedies for common ailments.

The most famous villages for these *Bauerngärten*, are Trub, Heimiswil and Sumiswald, all in the Emmental region, but for a double-whammy of visits, go to Koppigen, where you'll see lots of these beautiful cottage gardens, as well as the magnificent Oeschberg Horticultural School (page 59) – all in the same afternoon!

12 JARDIN BOTANIQUE FRIBOURG

Having just reached its half-century, this garden has plenty to celebrate with an established arboretum, ponds and glasshouses full of interesting plants. My favourite part of this garden is the collection of dessert apples, providing pretty blossom in spring and wonderful fruit in autumn. These varieties were very important locally, at times when sugar sources were scarce, and the names give plenty of clues as to quite how local they are, like the lovely "Douce Blanche de Botterens".

Dieser Garten, der gerade ein halbes Jahrhundert alt geworden ist, hat viel zu feiern mit seinem etablierten Arboretum sowie seinen Teichen und Gewächshäusern voller interessanter Pflanzen. Mein Lieblingsabschnitt in diesem Garten ist das Areal mit Dessertäpfeln, die im Frühjahr hübsche Blüten und im Herbst tolle Früchte tragen. Diese Sorten waren hierzulande sehr wichtig, als die Zuckerquellen knapp waren. Ihre Namen lassen viele Rückschlüsse zu, woher die Sorten genau stammen, wie z. B. der wundervolle ‹Douce Blanche de Botterens›.

Ayant atteint un demi-siècle il y a peu, ce jardin a largement de quoi célébrer, n'étant pas en reste avec son arboretum, ses étangs et ses serres remplies de plantes intéressantes. La chose que je préfère dans ce jardin est sa collection de pommes de table – les pommiers offrent des fleurs magnifiques au printemps, se transformant en de superbes fruits en automne. Ces différentes variétés étaient très importantes pour la région, au temps où les sources de sucre étaient rares – d'ailleurs, leurs noms donnent des indices sur leur caractère local, comme la charmante « Douce Blanche de Botterens ».

ADDRESS: Chemin du Musée 10, 1700 Fribourg

TRANSPORT: Bus 1, 3,9 stop Charmettes, Bus 7 stop Jardin Botanique

VISITOR INFORMATION: Opening hours are April–October 8–18, November to March weekdays 8–17, weekends 10–17

HIGHLIGHTS: There is lots to see in this small garden; don't miss the fragrant pelargoniums in summer.

13 CHÂTEAU DE GRUYÈRES

Overlooking the postcard-perfect village of Gruyères, this tiny formal garden is set against the dramatic landscape of the Dent de Broc and the Dent de Chamoix. It consists of a beautifully-maintained French parterre, and a number of heritage apple and pear varieties grown along the walls. Like most castle gardens, the parterre was designed to be seen from the balcony above, but make sure you get up close to the colourful and fragrant plantings inside the perfectly clipped box hedges.

Mit Blick auf das Bilderbuchdorf Greyerz hebt sich dieser kleine Barockgarten von der dramatischen Berglandschaft des Dent de Broc und Dent de Chamoix im Hintergrund ab. Er besteht aus einem wunderschön gepflegten französischen Parterre und einer Reihe von historischen Apfel- und Birnensorten, die entlang der Schlossmauern wachsen. Wie die meisten Schlossgärten wurde das Parterre so gestaltet, dass man es vom Balkon aus sehen kann, aber Sie sollten sich den bunten und duftenden Pflanzen inmitten der perfekt geschnittenen Buchsbaumhecken unbedingt auch nähern.

Donnant sur Gruyères, célèbre village à l'aspect digne d'une carte postale, ce petit jardin classique est niché dans un paysage somptueux au pied des deux voisines que sont la Dent de Broc et la Dent de Chamoix. Il est constitué d'un magnifique parterre à la française et d'anciennes variétés de pommes et de poires cultivées le long des murs. Comme la plupart des jardins de château, le parterre fut conçu pour être vu du balcon, mais ne manquez surtout pas de le voir de plus près afin d'observer toute la beauté de ses plantes colorées et parfumées se trouvant au cœur de buis taillés à la perfection.

ADDRESS: Rue du Château 8, 1663 Gruyères

TRANSPORT: Gruyères bus 263, plus a short walk to the castle

VISITOR INFORMATION: Museum opening hours are 9–6 in summer and 10–17 in winter. Garden opening months are spring to autumn.

HIGHLIGHTS: Garden access is free for disabled visitors

Swiss Gardens Schweiz/Suisse/Switzerland

14 ROSERAIE D'ESTAVAYER-LE-LAC

Estavayer-le-Lac is sometimes called "The City of the Rose", and with good reason. There are flowerbeds of the noble flower throughout the city, with a glorious collection of them below the castle walls. The rose garden is spaced out along a gentle walkway by the lake, like pearls strung on a necklace, and each large planting is beautifully maintained and well-labelled. Sturdy wooden arches provide shade for visitors as well as support for the dozens of climbing roses. The city walls and castle provide a beautiful backdrop for your photographs; it's just a pity they can't capture the perfume, too.

Estavayer-le-Lac wird manchmal aus gutem Grund ‹die Stadt der Rose› genannt. In der ganzen Stadt gibt es Blumenbeete mit dieser edlen Blume, mit einer prächtigen Ansammlung von ihnen am Fusse der Schlossmauern. Der Rosengarten erstreckt sich wie eine Perlenkette einen leichten Spazierweg um den See entlang und jede grosse Anpflanzung ist sowohl wunderbar gepflegt als auch gut beschriftet. Stabile Holzbögen spenden den Besuchern Schatten und stützen Dutzende von Kletterrosen. Die Stadtmauern und das Schloss bieten eine schöne Kulisse für Ihre Fotos – nur zu schade, dass man darauf nicht auch den Duft einfangen kann.

Estavayer-le-Lac est parfois nommée « Cité à la Rose », et ce à juste titre. La ville toute entière est décorée de parterres avec la fleur légendaire, une splendide collection se trouvant au pied des murs du château. Le jardin de roses est dispersé le long d'un chemin près du lac, tel un collier de perles, et chaque rosier est joliment entretenu et orné d'un écriteau. De solides arches en bois offrent de l'ombre aux visiteurs et soutiennent les douzaines de rosiers grimpants. Les murs et le château de la ville garantissent un magnifique arrière-plan pour vos photos – quel dommage que ces dernières ne puissent également saisir le parfum de cette noble fleur.

ADDRESS: Route de la Plage, Estavayer-le-Lac 1470

TRANSPORT: Estavayer-le-Lac train station, also buses 551, 552, 553, 554, 555 plus a short walk

VISITOR INFORMATION: Access to the rose garden is all day, every year.

HIGHLIGHTS: The rose garden is in bloom from early May to October.

15 LAUTREJARDIN

The founder of this show garden and nursery, Xavier Allemann, created it in 2005, well before the widespread development of the New Perennials Movement. When you arrive at the nursery, you'll see the front slope in front of the farmhouse is heaving with interesting and different plants, and you're just as likely to see Xavier here himself, planting, transplanting or just standing back and planning the next steps for the arrangement. Head up the path under the low arch and you'll find yourself in a different world. With modern perennial borders packed with old favourites and new friends, you're bound to be enchanted. For the plantophile, bring your notebook and your wallet; you're sure to go home with lots of ideas and plants.

Der Gründer dieses Schaugartens mit Baumschule, Xavier Allemann, legte ihn im Jahre 2005 an, also lange bevor das ‹New Perennials Movement› weite Verbreitung fand. Kommt man bei der Baumschule an, wimmelt es am vorderen Hang vor dem Bauernhaus vor interessanten und unterschiedlichen Pflanzen, und man trifft womöglich auf Xavier selbst beim Pflanzen, Umpflanzen oder auch einfach nur beim Betrachten und Planen der nächsten Schritte für die Ausgestaltung. Nimmt man den Pfad unter dem niedrigen Bogen hinauf, findet man sich in einer anderen Welt wieder: Moderne mehrjährige Borders voller alter Favoriten und neuer Lieblinge werden Sie hier verzaubern. Pflanzenliebhaber sollten ihr Notizbuch und ihre Geldbörse mitbringen, denn man geht mit Sicherheit mit vielen Ideen und Pflanzen nach Hause.

À la fois jardin d'exposition et pépinière, lautrejardin fut créé par Xavier Allemann en 2005, bien avant que le « New Perennial Movement » ne gagne en popularité. En arrivant à la pépinière, vous verrez que la pente avant est remplie de diverses plantes intéressantes, et il est fort probable que vous voyiez Xavier en personne, en train de planter, de rempoter ou de contempler l'aménagement en réfléchissant aux prochaines étapes de sa création. Empruntez le chemin sous l'arche qui vous mènera dans un autre monde. Vous allez être enchanté par les bordures de plantes vivaces modernes, remplies de variétés bien connues et aussi de nouveautés. Pour les mordus de végétaux, n'oubliez surtout pas votre carnet et votre portefeuille, car c'est avec de nombreuses plantes et idées que vous rentrerez chez vous.

ADDRESS: Chemin des Pontets 5, 1721 Cormérod

TRANSPORT: Cormérod, village buses 544 and 545

VISITOR INFORMATION: Opening hours March–November are Thursday/Friday 10–12, 13:30–17:30, plus Saturday 10–12 and 13:30–16. December–February call in advance.

HIGHLIGHTS: The bat garden at dusk is otherworldly and the big springtime colour explosion is phenomenal.

Swiss Gardens Schweiz/Suisse/Switzerland

16 MUSÉE DE L'ART ET HISTOIRE

This garden is something of a surprise, in the middle of one of Fribourg's oldest and most elegant neighbourhoods – it's a riot of colour and texture. Instead of heading up the steps into the museum, take a sharp right and go into the small but perfectly-formed lower garden. Box hedges line the rose-filled beds, and bright seasonal plantings bring the chromatic pace up another notch. The Niki de Saint Phalle sculpture, *La Grande Lune*, is the perfect match for this cheerful and irreverent mix. Don't forget to go through the gate to the secret garden to the side: there are more wonders in there.

Dieser Garten überrascht inmitten eines der ältesten und elegantesten Viertel von Freiburg – eine Explosion der Farben und Strukturen. Anstatt die Treppe zum Museum hinaufzusteigen, biegt man scharf rechts ab und gelangt dann in den kleinen, aber perfekt angelegten unteren Garten. Buchsbaumhecken säumen die rosengefüllten Beete und leuchtende saisonale Anpflanzungen verstärken das chromatische Farbenspiel. Die Skulptur von Niki de Saint Phalle, *La Grande Lune*, passt perfekt zu dieser fröhlichen und frechen Mischung. Nicht vergessen, durch das Tor zum seitlichen geheimen Garten zu gehen – darin sind noch mehr Wunder verborgen.

Ce jardin est une petite surprise, se situant en plein milieu d'un des plus vieux et des plus élégants quartiers de Fribourg – c'est une explosion de couleurs et de textures. Au lieu de suivre le chemin qui mène au musée, prenez directement à droite et dirigez-vous vers le jardin en contrebas, petit mais formé de manière parfaite. Des haies de buis longent les massifs de roses et des plantes saisonnières de couleurs éclatantes font monter d'un cran le jeu chromatique du jardin. *La Grande Lune* de Niki de Saint Phalle est la sculpture idéale pour ce mélange joyeux et excentrique. N'oubliez pas de franchir le portail afin de visiter le jardin secret se trouvant sur le côté – davantage de merveilles vous y attendent.

ADDRESS: Rue de Morat 12, CH 1700 Fribourg

TRANSPORT: Fribourg Tilleul buses 1,2,6,123,124,127,181,182, M17, N1, N5 and a short walk or Capucins bus 1 or N5

VISITOR INFORMATION: Open all day, very day

HIGHLIGHTS: Sculptures, great planting and an amazing view combine to make this small garden worth a detour.

Swiss Gardens Schweiz/Suisse/Switzerland

17 PAPILIORAMA

Part magical butterfly kingdom, part tropical paradise, part Swiss fauna reserve, this is an unusual garden by any standards. The heart of the complex is the butterfly dome, tilted to maximise the available light, and packed with tropical species to support the butterfly population with egg-laying, feeding and places to take a rest. Dozens of different palms, lots of nectar-rich flowers and a comfortable ambient temperature means that this is a great place to visit summer or winter. The tropical garden, a miniature copy of the Papiliorama Foundation's protected reserve in Belize, is a treasure trove of productive and powerful plants, including mangroves and orchids.

Teils magisches Schmetterlingsreich, teils tropisches Paradies, teils Reservat der Schweizer Fauna, ist das Papiliorama in jeder Hinsicht ein ungewöhnlicher Garten. Das Herzstück des Komplexes ist die Schmetterlingskuppel, deren Neigung das verfügbare Licht maximiert und die mit tropischen Arten bepflanzt ist, um die Schmetterlingspopulation beim Eierlegen, Fressen und Ausruhen zu unterstützen. Dutzende von verschiedenen Palmen, viele nektarreiche Blumen und eine angenehme Umgebungstemperatur machen diesen Ort zu einem idealen Ausflugsziel im Sommer und im Winter. Der tropische Garten, eine Miniaturkopie des geschützten Naturschutzareals der Papiliorama-Stiftung in Belize, ist eine Fundgrube für produktive und leistungsstarke Pflanzen wie Mangroven und Orchideen.

Ce jardin est tout à fait unique en son genre, étant à la fois le royaume magique des papillons, un paradis tropical et une petite réserve de la faune suisse. Le cœur du complexe est le dôme consacré aux papillons, incliné de manière à optimiser la lumière naturelle et rempli d'espèces tropicales afin de soutenir ces insectes au cours de leur cycle de vie, leur offrant de la nourriture ainsi que des coins où pondre et où se reposer. Avec ses dizaines de palmiers différents, ses fleurs riches en nectar et son agréable température ambiante, cet endroit est idéal pour une visite en été tout comme en hiver. Le Jungle Trek, une copie miniature de la zone protégée par la Fondation Papiliorama au Belize, une mine de trésors, regorgeant entre autres de plantes vigoureuses, y compris des mangroves et des orchidées.

ADDRESS: Moosmatte 1, 3210 Kerzers

TRANSPORT: Papiliorama train stop

VISITOR INFORMATION: Tickets cost 19 CHF for adults, 9.50 for children aged 4 to 15, free for children under 3. Opening hours 9–18 in summer and 10–17 in winter.

HIGHLIGHTS: More than just a butterfly garden, this is a brilliant family day out including bats, sloths and lots of glorious tropical plants.

A LAND OF ROSES

According to the World Federation of Roses, Switzerland has more rose gardens per capita than any other major European nation. This might seem surprising, but according to the rose specialist Alain Tschanz, based near Lausanne, this is because the Swiss continental climate is just perfect for these beautiful flowers: just enough rain, but not too much, and just the right amount of heat in summer. Although the choice of roses declines as altitude of the garden increases – and very few of them thrive above 1700m – there is still a rose variety for almost every garden and situation. Roses thrive on tiny Zurich balconies and on large country estates in Canton Vaud and it is this variation in climate and geography that gives this small country such a huge breadth of plant choice.

Rosen Huber is a Dottikon-based rose breeder, established in 1948 (see page 87) and has a large collection of special Swiss roses, named after famous Swiss people, or places. One of their most popular "people" roses is "Doris Leuthard," named for the ex-President of the Confederation, which has unusual pale pink petals with a sheen of orange, and a strong fragrance, with notes of citrus and lychee.

If you don't have space for a rose in your own garden, why not visit some of the incredible rose gardens in Switzerland? There are several in this book, as well as many gardens that include rose collections. It's always good to stop and smell the roses.

Rose gardens
- Rosengarten in Bern (page 61)
- Roseraie Thérèse Mayer in Estavayer (page 41)
- Schloss Heidegg (page 91)
- Au Diable Vert (page 19)
- Roseraie de la Vallée de la Jeunesse, 1007 Lausanne
- Rosengarten, Hochwachtstrasse, 8400 Winterthur

Gardens with significant rose collections
- Arboretum National du Vallon de l'Aubonne (page 17)

Rose growers
- Huber Roses, Dottikon (page 87)
- Alain Tschanz, Roses Anciennes, route de Bussigny 1, 1123 Aclens
- Olivier Tschanz, Roses Passion, Roseraies Tschanz SA, Rte de Villars-sous-Yens 4B, 1162 St-Prex

18 ALPENGARTEN SCHYNIGE PLATTE

If a garden could win a prize for being the most fun and picturesque to get to, then this would be a world-beater. The cog railway that pulls the little carriages up from Wilderswil travels through forest and meadows – and the entrance fee to the garden is included in the price of a train ticket. Most visitors only stay half an hour here and then carry on with their hike, but you can easily lose several hours here, wandering round the paths. You can spot most of the Alpine favourites, like gentians and edelweiss on the shorter circuit, but if you're a plant lover, allow several hours to explore the rest – with the chance to see majority of all Alpine flora at once.

Wenn ein Garten einen Preis dafür bekäme, der auf die lustigste und malerischste Art erreichbare Garten zu sein, dann gewänne dieser sicherlich. Die Zahnradbahn, die die kleinen Wagons von Wilderswil den Berg hochzieht, fährt durch Wald und Wiesen – und der Eintritt zum Garten ist im Preis der Bahnfahrkarte enthalten. Die meisten Besucher bleiben nur eine halbe Stunde dort und setzen dann ihre Wanderung fort, aber man kann leicht mehrere Stunden auf den Pfaden wandernd im Garten verbringen. Auf den kürzeren Rundgängen bekommt man die meisten alpinen Favoriten wie Enziane und Edelweiss zu sehen, aber wenn man Pflanzenliebhaber ist, sollte man mehrere Stunden einplanen, um den Rest zu erkunden. Dann hat man die Chance, einen Grossteil der gesamten Alpenflora an einem Tag sichten zu können.

Si un jardin pouvait remporter le prix du jardin à l'accès le plus amusant et le plus pittoresque, celui-ci serait sans aucun doute le gagnant. Le train à crémaillère qui tire les petits wagons depuis Wilderswil voyage à travers la forêt et les prés – le billet d'entrée du jardin est inclus dans le prix du billet de train. La plupart des visiteurs ne restent qu'une petite demi-heure et continuent ensuite leur randonnée, mais vous pouvez aisément y passer des heures à flâner sur les sentiers. En empruntant le chemin le plus court, vous découvrirez un grand nombre de fleurs alpines, comme la gentiane ou l'edelweiss, mais si vous êtes un véritable amoureux des plantes, comptez plusieurs heures pour explorer le reste – avec la chance de voir la majorité de la flore alpine au cours d'une seule excursion.

ADDRESS: Bergstation Schynige Platte-Bahn, 3812 Wilderswil

TRANSPORT: Schynige Platte

VISITOR INFORMATION: Opening hours 8.30 to 18, from end May to end October. Entry price is included in the train ticket.

HIGHLIGHTS: Alpine enthusiasts and amateur plant-lovers alike will love this garden. Guided tours are available on request.

19 BOTANISCHER GARTEN DER UNIVERSITÄT BERN

Come in under the grand arch on the Lorrainebrücke, walk down the steps, and the sound of the traffic magically disappears. You are in another world. Birdsong, the river rushing by, and humming bees replace the urgent modernity above you on the bridge. Enjoy the different pace here and take a tour of the world in plants. Amble from the Alps, to the Mediterranean, to the tropics, pausing to admire an edelweiss here or a palm tree there. Or to submit to the atmosphere of calm contemplation, find a bench to sit on and enjoy the turquoise Aare rushing past and the gentle buzzing of the bees.

Tritt man durch den grossen Bogen der Lorrainebrücke in den Garten und läuft die Treppe hinunter, ist der Verkehrslärm wie von Zauberhand verschwunden. Man ist in einer anderen Welt. Vogelgesang, der vorbei fliessende Fluss und summende Bienen ersetzen die aufdringliche Moderne oben auf der Brücke. Geniessen Sie das andere Tempo hier und unternehmen Sie einen Rundgang durch die Welt der Pflanzen. Schlendern Sie von den Alpen über den Mittelmeerraum in die Tropen und halten Sie inne, um hier ein Edelweiss oder dort eine Palme zu bewundern. Oder Sie geben sich ganz und gar dem Ambiente der ruhigen Besinnung hin, suchen sich eine Bank zum Hinsetzen und geniessen das vorbeirauschende Türkis der Aare sowie das sanfte Summen der Bienen.

Passez sous le grand arc du pont de Lorraine, descendez les escaliers, et le bruit routier va soudainement disparaître, comme par magie, vous plongeant dans un autre monde. Le chant des oiseaux, les douces notes du cours d'eau et le bourdonnement des abeilles remplacent le bruit de la vie moderne et envahissante se déroulant au-dessus de vous. Profitez du rythme plus calme de cet endroit et faites un tour du monde des plantes : promenez-vous des Alpes à la Méditerranée en passant par les tropiques, parsemant le tout de petites pauses pour admirer, ici et là, un edelweiss ou encore un palmier. Vous pouvez aussi vous immerger dans cette atmosphère de contemplation sereine, trouver un banc sur lequel vous asseoir et contempler les eaux turquoise de l'Aar bercées par le murmure des abeilles.

ADDRESS: Altenbergrain 21, 3013 Bern
TRANSPORT: Bus 20, Gewerbeschule

VISITOR INFORMATION: Opening hours 8–17:30 March-September, shorter hours in winter, check website

HIGHLIGHTS: A quiet haven in the city, a short walk from the station. Great workshops for kids, too.

20 GARTENPFLANZEN DAEPP

This is the first "experience nursery" in Switzerland – perhaps in the world. The idea is that you walk around and enjoy yourself, take a seat, enjoy the view, smell the roses. In short, all the things that bring pleasure in a garden, but it's all in a garden centre. If you want to buy a plant, you just have to ask, and if you want advice, there are plenty of knowledgeable Daepp team members to help. This family firm have existed since 1857, and this new way of showing plants won them the garden centre of the year in 2018 – not a bad way to celebrate your 161st birthday.

Dies ist die erste ‹Erlebnis-Baumschule› der Schweiz oder vielleicht sogar der Welt. Die Idee dahinter ist, spazieren zu gehen und alles zu erleben, sich hinzusetzen, die Aussicht zu geniessen und den Duft der Rosen einzuatmen. Kurz gesagt, all die Dinge zu tun, die bei einem Gartenbesuch Freude machen, nur hier gibt es das alles in einem Gartencenter. Wenn man eine Pflanze kaufen möchte, muss man nur danach fragen, und wenn man Beratung wünscht, gibt es viele sachkundige Daepp-Teammitglieder, die Ihnen gerne weiterhelfen. Das Familienunternehmen gibt es seit 1857. Es wurde 2018 mit dieser neuen Art der Pflanzenpräsentation zum Gartencenter des Jahres gekürt – keine schlechte Art, seinen 161. Geburtstag zu feiern.

Il s'agit de la toute première « pépinière expérimentale » de Suisse, peut-être même du monde. Le principe consiste à s'y promener et à se détendre, s'asseoir, admirer la vue, humer les roses. En bref, à profiter de toutes les choses agréables d'un jardin, sauf qu'ici, tout se trouve dans une jardinerie. Si vous voulez acheter une plante, vous n'avez qu'à demander – les nombreux membres du personnel de Daepp, tous très compétents, sont là pour vous conseiller. Cette entreprise familiale existe depuis 1857 et cette manière innovatrice d'exposer les plantes leur a permis de remporter le prix de la jardinerie de l'année 2018 – pas mal pour célébrer son 161e anniversaire.

ADDRESS: Bärenstutz 7, 3110 Münsingen

TRANSPORT: Bus 162, Munsingen Bärenstutz

VISITOR INFORMATION: The shop opening hours are Mon-Friday 9–17, Saturday 8–16, Sunday closed but there is free access to the garden.

HIGHLIGHTS: Don't miss the flowering of the rhododendrons, March to May.

21 ELFENAU PARK

Gardens, like anything else, fall under the spell of the sorcery of fashion, and the Elfenau Park is no exception. From its monastic origins, the park has seen baroque geometry come and go, and we are left with a perfect example of the English Landscape Park, with rolling lawns, hills and carefully-framed views. The beautiful River Aare, mostly out of sight from the house and upper garden, is easily reached with gentle strolls past the centennial trees. The new ProSpecieRara garden provides a fantastic splash of colour in the upper reaches of the garden with heritage varieties of perennials and annuals.

Gärten unterliegen, wie alles andere, dem Bann der Modeerscheinungen und der Elfenau Park bildet da keine Ausnahme. Durch seine Ursprünge als Kloster hat der Park seine barocke Geometrie kommen und gehen sehen, und nun liegt hier ein perfektes Beispiel für einen englischen Landschaftspark mit sanft geschwungenen Rasenflächen, Hügeln und sorgfältig eingerahmten Ausblicken. Der schöne Fluss Aare, meist vom Haus und dem Obergarten aus nicht zu sehen, ist mit einem Spaziergang vorbei an den hundertjährigen Bäumen leicht zu erreichen. Der neue ProSpecieRara-Garten sorgt im oberen Teil des Gartens für fantastische Farbtupfer mit historischen Varianten der mehr- und einjährigen Pflanzen.

Les jardins aussi, comme toute autre chose, peuvent être des victimes de la mode – et le parc de l'Elfenau n'y échappe pas. Depuis ses origines monastiques, ce parc a connu plusieurs époques de formes géométriques baroques. À présent, il s'agit d'un exemple parfait de parc paysager de style anglais, avec des pelouses verdoyantes, de jolies collines et des vues subtilement dégagées. Le magnifique fleuve de l'Aar, que l'on ne voit pratiquement pas depuis la maison et la partie supérieure du jardin, est facilement accessible après une petite balade vous menant au-delà des arbres centenaires. Le nouveau jardin ProSpecieRara exhibe des couleurs éclatantes dans ses parties les plus hautes, agrémentées de variétés traditionnelles de fleurs vivaces et annuelles.

ADDRESS: Elfenauweg 92, 3006 Bern TRANSPORT: Bus Luternauerweg 19, M4	VISITOR INFORMATION: Free to visit all day, every day	HIGHLIGHTS: A huge park, perfect for family strolling, with great views down to the Aare

22 OESCHBERG GARTENBAUSCHULE

The Oeschberg horticultural school was founded in 1920, and the park and gardens were finished in 1932. The formal gardens close to the house – a listed building – are a perfect example of 1930s garden design with a sunken pool as well as an arbour covered in climbing plants. Below the formal gardens are the students' teaching beds: full of colour and interest all year round, from the earliest spring bulbs to autumn sedums and grasses for winter. The park includes specimen trees as well as a rhododendron dell and rockeries.

Die Gartenbauschule Oeschberg wurde 1920 gegründet, der Park und die Gärten im Jahre 1932 fertiggestellt. Die Barockgärten in der Nähe des Hauses – einem denkmalgeschützten Gebäude – sind ein perfektes Beispiel für die Gartengestaltung der 1930er Jahre mit einem eingebetteten Teich sowie einer mit Kletterpflanzen bedeckten Laube. Unterhalb der Barockgärten befinden sich die Lehrbeete der Schüler. Sie sind das ganze Jahr über bunt und interessant: von den frühesten Zwiebelgewächsen im Frühling bis hin zum Sedum im Herbst und den Wintergräsern. Der Park zeigt Solitärbäume sowie eine Rhododendronsenke und Steingärten.

L'école d'horticulture d'Oeschberg fut fondée en 1920 et le parc ainsi que les jardins furent achevés en 1932. Les jardins classiques près de la maison – classée monument historique – sont une parfaite illustration des jardins des années 30, accompagnés d'un bassin à débordement ainsi que d'une tonnelle sur laquelle fleurissent des plantes grimpantes. Plus bas se trouvent les parterres avec lesquels les étudiants s'exercent, remplis tout au long de l'année de plantes aussi intéressantes que multicolores : bulbes de printemps, sedums automnaux et herbes en hiver. Le parc comprend aussi des arbres dominant le paysage ainsi que des rhododendrons et des rocailles.

ADDRESS: Bern-Zürich-Strasse 14, 3425 Koppigen

TRANSPORT: Oeschberg 466 bus

VISITOR INFORMATION: Free acess to visitors all year, every day

HIGHLIGHTS: A large and varied park with formal gardens, botanical family groups and beautiful seasonal planting

23 ROSENGARTEN BERN

Would you like to take a picture of yourself with one of the most famous past residents of the city, Albert Einstein? Climb the steps here, and near the collection of historic roses, you'll find a bronze statue of the physicist, with a space next to him, just right for taking selfies. Head on up the hill to the lawns and you'll find the best view in the city, over the bears and rooftops to the cathedral and the parliament buildings. There's much more to enjoy than just roses, with a superb rhododendron collection, thousands of confetti-like crocuses in spring, and lots of lush lawns to lie on in summer.

Möchten Sie ein Foto mit einem der berühmtesten ehemaligen Bewohner der Stadt, Albert Einstein? Steigt man hier die Treppe hinauf, trifft man in der Nähe der historischen Rosensammlung auf eine Bronzestatue des Physikers und daneben etwas Platz, genau richtig für ein Selfie mit ihm. Geht man den Hügel hinauf zu den Rasenflächen, findet man den besten Blick auf die Stadt vor, über die Bären und Dächer hinweg bis hin zum Münster und den Parlamentsgebäuden. Es gibt viel mehr zu sehen als nur Rosen, mit einer grossartigen Ansammlung an Rhododendren, Tausenden von konfettiartig verstreuten Krokussen im Frühjahr und vielen üppigen Rasenflächen, auf denen man im Sommer die Sonne geniessen kann.

Aimeriez-vous vous prendre en photo avec l'un des plus célèbres anciens habitants de la ville, Albert Einstein ? Empruntez la pente raide et vous trouverez une statue de bronze à l'effigie du physicien à côté de la collection de roses anciennes – vous pouvez vous asseoir à côté de lui pour prendre des selfies. Allez au sommet de la colline, jusqu'aux pelouses, et vous aurez la chance de pouvoir profiter de la plus belle vue de la ville, au-dessus des ours et des toits bernois, donnant sur la cathédrale et sur le Palais fédéral. Il y a bien plus encore que des roses : une superbe collection de rhododendrons, des milliers de crocus au printemps, parsemés tels des confettis de toutes les couleurs, et de grandes pelouses luxuriantes sur lesquelles s'allonger en été.

ADDRESS: Alter Aargauerstalden 31B, 3006 Bern TRANSPORT: Rosengarten buses 10, 40, M3	VISITOR INFORMATION: Opening hours all day and every day	HIGHLIGHTS: Spring visits to enjoy the crocuses and daffodils, and summer visits for the roses. Any time for the view.

Swiss Gardens Schweiz/Suisse/Switzerland

24 SCHLOSS BÜMPLIZ

This is a castle on a human scale, meant to be lived in and enjoyed, and the modestly-sized but charming gardens are a reflection of that. The front lawns come alive in spring with thousands of daffodils and then the focus moves on to the walled garden. Locals come and sit at the tables in the garden and enjoy the box-edged beds full of annuals battling it out for supremacy with the wisteria, grapevine and roses. The park to the rear provides shade and places to sit and think, with several centenary trees and a large formal pond.

Dieses Schloss zeugt von menschlicher Grösse, war zum Wohnen und Geniessen bestimmt, was die kleinen aber charmanten Gärten widerspiegeln. Die vorderen Rasenflächen erwachen im Frühling mit Tausenden von Narzissen zum Leben und dann rückt der ummauerte Garten in den Mittelpunkt. Die Einheimischen kommen zu Besuch, setzen sich an die Tische im Garten und geniessen die kastenförmigen Beete voller einjähriger Pflanzen, wo Blauregen, Weinreben und Rosen um die Vorherrschaft ringen. Der hintere Teil des Parks spendet Schatten und bietet Orte zum Hinsetzen und Nachdenken mit seinen mehreren hundertjährigen Bäumen und einem grossen angelegten Teich.

Ce château fut construit pour y vivre et pour y profiter de la vie, et les jardins, certes pas très grands mais tout à fait charmants, l'illustrent parfaitement. Les pelouses à l'avant resplendissent au printemps, période durant laquelle elles sont remplies de milliers de jonquilles – plus loin, l'attention est portée sur le jardin clos. Les gens du coin viennent s'asseoir aux tables afin de jouir de la vue sur les plates-bandes garnies de fleurs annuelles et ceinturées de buis, côtoyant les glycines, les vignes et les roses, toutes plus belles les unes que les autres. À l'arrière, le parc offre de l'ombre ainsi que des endroits où s'asseoir et laisser ses pensées vagabonder, en compagnie de plusieurs arbres centenaires et d'un grand étang de style classique.

ADDRESS: Bümplizstrasse 97, 3018 Bern	VISITOR INFORMATION: Visiting hourse from dawn to dusk, every day.	HIGHLIGHTS: The seasonal bedding in the walled garden is always sensational, and the park is a quiet place for contemplation.
TRANSPORT: Bümpliz, Schloss bus 27		

Swiss Gardens Schweiz/Suisse/Switzerland

25 STAUDENGARTEN SCHULZ

An unassuming village in the Bernese countryside is host to a small but perfectly-formed perennials garden. Ancient apple trees give rhythm and structure to the soft and luxurious planting, and occasional gaps in the perimeter allow views to the fields and woods beyond. Like most perennial gardens, this is at its best from May onwards, with a spectacular period in early autumn when the softer light combines with the seedheads and late-summer flowers to make something magical. The garden is surrounded by the ecologically-minded community, including a farm shop, café full of local produce, and a working farm.

Ein unauffälliges Dorf im Kanton Bern beherbergt einen kleinen, aber perfekt gestalteten Garten mit mehrjährigen Pflanzen. Uralte Apfelbäume verleihen der zarten und edlen Bepflanzung Rhythmus und Struktur. Gelegentliche Lücken in der Gartenabgrenzung ermöglichen den Blick auf die dahinterliegenden Felder und Wälder. Wie die meisten mehrjährigen Gärten ist dieser Garten ab Mai am schönsten, gefolgt von einer spektakulären Periode im Frühherbst, wenn das weichere Licht sich mit dem Fruchtstand und Spätsommerblumen zu etwas Magischem verbindet. Der Garten ist von einer ökologisch orientierten Gemeinschaft umgeben, zu der ein Bauernladen, ein Café mit lokalen Produkten und ein Bauernhof gehören.

Un village sans prétention au sein de la campagne bernoise accueille ce petit jardin formé à la perfection et rempli de plantes vivaces. Des pommiers anciens apportent une structure harmonieuse aux plantations à la fois délicates et luxuriantes, et les quelques ouvertures permettent de jouir des vues donnant sur les champs et les bois se trouvant plus loin. Comme la plupart des jardins vivaces, il connaît son apogée à partir du mois de mai, mais aussi une magnifique période au début de l'automne, lorsque la lumière douce se pose sur les porte-graines et les fleurs, créant une ambiance enchanteresse. Le jardin est entouré d'une communauté à l'esprit écologique, y compris une boutique agricole, un café plein de produits de la région et une ferme.

ADDRESS: 36 Schüpfenried, 3043 Uttligen

TRANSPORT: Uettligen, Schüpfenried 102, M8

VISITOR INFORMATION: Opening hours are all day from sunrise to sunset, all year

HIGHLIGHTS: The springtime spectacular starts in May and runs until July; don't miss the autumn show from September to November.

26 TROPENHAUS

Best known for the magnificent scenery and fabulous train ride through the tunnels to Italy, the region also boasts another, considerably warmer attraction. Using the warm water pumped out of the Lötschberg tunnel, the greenhouses produce a couple of tonnes of exotic fruit per year – as well as managing a thriving aquaculture. You'll find papayas, pineapples and orchids as well as a fun and educational introduction to farming tropical commodities like coffee. You can buy fruit and fish in the shop, or try them in the restaurant. This is a perfect winter outing combining a tropical experience and an ecological education, all in the warm indoors.

Bekannt für die herrliche Landschaft und die fabelhafte Zugfahrt durch die Tunnel nach Italien, verfügt die Region auch über eine weitere, wesentlich wärmere Attraktion. Mit dem aus dem Lötschbergtunnel gepumpten Warmwasser produzieren die Gewächshäuser jährlich einige Tonnen exotisches Obst und betreiben eine blühende Aquakultur. Hier gibt es Papayas, Ananas und Orchideen sowie eine spassige und lehrreiche Einführung in die tropische Rohstoffproduktion wie etwa von Kaffee. Man kann Obst und Fisch im Laden kaufen oder im Restaurant probieren. Ein perfekter Winterausflug, der ein tropisches Erlebnis mit ökologischer Bildung verbindet, und das alles geschützt vor der Kälte.

Surtout connue pour sa vue imprenable et son fabuleux voyage en train – celui-ci traverse les tunnels jusqu'en Italie – la région comprend une attraction supplémentaire, proposant des températures plus élevées. Grâce à l'eau chaude provenant du tunnel du Lötschberg, les serres produisent quelques tonnes de fruits exotiques par an et maintiennent une aquaculture florissante. Vous trouverez des papayes, des ananas et des orchidées ainsi que des informations utiles et divertissantes sur la manière de cultiver des produits exotiques comme le café. Le magasin vous permet d'acheter des fruits et du poisson – ou alors, vous pouvez y goûter au restaurant. C'est la parfaite sortie hivernale qui offre une aventure tropicale enrichie d'un côté didactique sur l'écologie, le tout en restant bien au chaud.

ADDRESS: Tropenhausweg 1, 3714 Frutigen

TRANSPORT: Bus Frutigen, Tropenhaus

VISITOR INFORMATION: Costs 18 CHF for adults, children aged 6–16 9 CHF, children under 6 free. Opening hours Tuesday–Saturday 9–23, Sunday 9–18, closed Monday except Bank Holidays. Open all year except 24, 25 December and annual closure 14–24 January

HIGHLIGHTS: Switzerland's only indoor tropical garden, perfect for when there's snow on the ground outside

ALPINE GARDENS

What could be more Swiss than an alpine garden? Actually, the craze for alpine gardens came much later to Switzerland than elsewhere in Europe. The first non-Swiss European alpine gardens were created by returning visitors who had fallen in love with the Alps, and wanted to remind themselves of the beautiful landscapes and plants they had seen there. You don't feel the same urge to plant an alpine garden when the real thing is all around you. However, visitors to Switzerland wanted to see the flowers they had come to see, and this, combined with a rising interest in conservation, meant that botanical alpine gardens were a logical next step. The turn of the century saw a flurry of new alpine gardens, with La Linnea in Bourg Saint Pierre founded in 1889, followed by La Thomasia in Pont-de-Nant in 1891, and La Rambertia in Les Rochers de Naye in 1896. The railway for the Schynige Platte (see page 51) opened in 1893, but they had to wait until 1927 to open the garden. All of these gardens are still open to the public, and are among the Top Ten Swiss alpine gardens.

The highest of these, at 2080m is the Alpengarten Aletsch, part of the Pro Natura visitor centre in Riederalp. You can stay in the visitor centre, and enjoy the garden before anyone else arrives. You can also do this at the Flore-Alpe garden in Champex, with the added benefit of the magnificent views onto Lac de Champex.

Growing your own alpine plants is surprisingly easy. They make the perfect plants for a small space, like a balcony or terrace, and many of them are so tiny that they benefit from being viewed at close quarters. They are the ideal plants for city dwellers, and you really don't need a special alpine trough, lovely as they are, to get the best from them. In nature, alpine plants usually grow above the tree line, and in their natural habitat have very well-drained soil with plenty of rocks and gravel. They can be bulbs, perennials and even woody plants, and generally bloom in the spring or summer. Sedums, saxifrages and aubrieta are cheap and easily found in most garden centres, and are unfussy plants, ideal for beginners. They will do very well in a container or a window box. Just check that your container has good drainage holes and mix in some gravel with the potting compost at planting time.

27 GARTEN HAUS WYSS

Wyss is not only one of Switzerland's oldest and most important seed companies, but the Zuchwil site is also one of the first modern garden centres in the country, opened in 1962. The Isler shell-structure building is itself unique, but the real attractions here are the horticultural wonders. The show park was planted in 1963 – intended to show potential purchasers how their trees were going to develop – and is now a mature park. The trials garden is a riot of colour and textures, where the company grow their own seeds and those of competitors to see if they will thrive in the Swiss climate. Both are open to the public.

Wyss ist nicht nur eines der ältesten und bedeutendsten Saatgutunternehmen der Schweiz, denn der im Jahre 1962 eröffnete Standort Zuchwil ist auch eines der ersten modernen Gartencenter des Landes. Das Isler Gebäude in Schalenstruktur ist schon an sich einzigartig, aber die wahren Attraktionen sind hier die gartenbaulichen Wunder. Der 1963 angepflanzte Schaugarten – der potenziellen Käufern zeigen sollte, wie sich ihre Bäume entwickeln können – ist heute ein voll entfalteter Park. Der Versuchsgarten ist eine Explosion an Farben und Strukturen, in dem das Unternehmen sein eigenes Saatgut und das der Konkurrenten anpflanzt, um zu sehen, ob sie im Schweizer Klima gedeihen. Beide sind für die Öffentlichkeit zugänglich.

Wyss est non seulement l'un des semenciers les plus vieux et parmi les plus importants du pays, mais le site de Zuchwill est aussi l'une des premières jardineries modernes du pays, ayant ouvert en 1962. La structure en coquille du bâtiment signée Heinz Isler est déjà unique en soi, mais les véritables attractions de ce lieu sont les merveilles du monde horticole que l'on y trouve. Le parc d'exposition fut fondé en 1963 dans le but de montrer aux potentiels acheteurs la manière dont leurs arbres vont grandir – à présent, c'est un parc rempli d'arbres matures. Dans le jardin expérimental, riche en couleurs et en textures, l'entreprise fait pousser ses propres graines ainsi que celles de ses concurrents afin de voir si elles prospèrent dans le climat suisse. Les deux sont ouverts au public.

ADDRESS: Gartenstrasse 32, CH 4528 Zuchwil

TRANSPORT: Zuchwil, Kornfeld bus 1, 5, 7, M11 or Zuchwil, Juraplatz bus 4,6,9

VISITOR INFORMATION: Opening hours are Mon–Fri 9–18:30 Sat 8–17, closed Bank Holidays.

HIGHLIGHTS: The park is great to visit any time of year – don't miss the trials fields in summer and the orchid show in late winter

28 BOTANISCHER GARTEN DER UNIVERSITÄT BASEL

Founded in 1460, Basel University is the oldest in Switzerland, and the botanical garden – created shortly afterwards – is one of the oldest in the world. It's small but perfectly formed, with all the treats you might expect to enjoy in a Swiss botanical garden. As well as the small alpine collection, there's a truly eclectic group of plant families, far from the usual "order bed" choices. The 1898 Viktoriahaus glasshouse still grows a number of the giant waterlilies for which it was originally named. There are also several superb centennial trees dotted around the garden, including a particularly attractive weeping beech.

Die 1460 gegründete Universität Basel ist die älteste der Schweiz und der kurz darauf angelegte Botanische Garten ist einer der ältesten der Welt. Er ist klein, aber perfekt gestaltet, mit allen besonderen Vergnügen, die man in einem Schweizer Botanischen Garten erwarten würde. Abgesehen von der kleinen alpinen Kollektion gibt es eine wahrhaft eklektische Gruppe von Pflanzenfamilien abseits der üblichen ‹Bestellbeet›-Auswahl. Im Gewächshaus ‹Viktoriahaus› von 1898 wächst noch eine Reihe der riesigen Seerosen, nach denen es ursprünglich benannt wurde. Im Garten stehen auch mehrere prächtige hundertjährige Bäume, darunter eine besonders attraktive Trauerbuche.

L'Université de Bâle fut fondée en 1460, ce qui fait d'elle la première université de Suisse, et le jardin botanique, créé peu après, est l'un des plus anciens du monde. Petit mais d'une forme parfaite, il offre tous les éléments plaisants que l'on attend d'un jardin botanique helvétique. En plus d'une petite collection alpine, il dispose d'un mélange éclectique de différentes familles de plantes, tout à fait hors du commun. La serre *Viktoriahaus* datant de 1898 continue d'abriter un certain nombre de nénuphars géants, qui lui ont d'ailleurs valu son nom. Le jardin est également parsemé de plusieurs arbres centenaires somptueux, dont un hêtre pleureur particulièrement beau.

ADDRESS: Spalengraben 8, 4051 Basel

TRANSPORT: Spalentor, bus 30

VISITOR INFORMATION: Opening hours April–October 8–18, November–March 8–17. Glasshouse opening times are shorter than those of the park.

HIGHLIGHTS: Don't miss the giant water lilies, in the Viktoriahaus

29 FONDATION BEYELER

The town of Riehen, separated from the city of Basel by a narrow strip of green, has managed to retain the charm of small-town Switzerland and offers not one but two magnificent gardens. The Fondation Beyeler is found on the main street in the town, and the Renzo Piano-designed building is surrounded by a park in miniature, including perfect lawns, water features and some particularly lovely specimen trees. The entire garden is maintained to an impeccable standard – not a blade of grass out of place – although apparently the smell of the fallen ginkgo fruit in autumn cannot be manicured-away in quite the same way.

Die Stadt Riehen, durch einen schmalen grünen Streifen von der Stadt Basel getrennt, hat sich den Charme einer schweizerischen Kleinstadt bewahrt und bietet nicht nur einen, sondern gleich zwei prächtige Gärten. Die Fondation Beyeler befindet sich an der Hauptstrasse der Stadt, und das von Renzo Piano entworfene Gebäude ist von einem Miniaturpark umgeben, der perfekte Rasenflächen, Wasserspiele und einige besonders schöne Solitärbäume umfasst. Der gesamte Garten ist tadellos in Schuss gehalten – kein Grashalm am falschen Ort – obwohl der Geruch der gefallenen Ginkgo-Frucht im Herbst nicht ebenso tadellos zu pflegen ist.

La commune de Riehen, séparée de la ville de Bâle par quelques petits terrains herbeux, a réussi à préserver le charme typique des petites villes helvétiques, et elle offre non pas un, mais deux magnifiques jardins. La Fondation Beyeler se trouve dans la rue principale et le bâtiment conçu par Renzo Piano est entouré d'un parc en miniature, composé de pelouses parfaites, de pièces d'eau et de quelques arbres d'une beauté particulièrement saisissante. L'ensemble du jardin est entretenu de manière impeccable – pas un seul brin d'herbe ne dépasse – mais il semble toutefois impossible de maintenir ce niveau exceptionnel avec le ginkgo, car on ne peut masquer l'odeur de ses fruits tombés en automne.

ADDRESS: Baselstrasse 101, 4125 Basel

TRANSPORT: Riehen Fondation Beyeler, tram 6

VISITOR INFORMATION: Opening hours 10–18 Monday–Sunday, Wednesday 10–20.

HIGHLIGHTS: The park is free to visit, and full of sculptures from the collection.

Swiss Gardens Schweiz/Suisse/Switzerland

30 WENKENPARK

Basel's favourite tennis-playing son, Roger Federer, chose this baroque beauty for his wedding in 2009, but rather than just being a playground for the rich and discreet of Basel, it's a fabulous mix of garden styles, and open to the public. The lower part of the garden is dominated by rolling lawns and grand stands of centennial trees, culminating in a small water-lily filled lake. Above it, you'll find the French Garden, often referred to as a "mini Versailles", but owing as much to the Dutch and Italian garden traditions as to the French formal style. The modern perennials garden nearby, with plants provided by ProSpecieRara, brings the mix of garden styles up to date.

Basels beliebtester Tennisspieler Roger Federer wählte diese barocke Schönheit als Ort für seine Hochzeit 2009. Der Park ist aber nicht nur ein Spielplatz für die Reichen und Diskreten Basels, sondern eine fabelhafte Mischung aus Gartenstilen – und öffentlich zugänglich. Der untere Teil des Gartens wird von hügeligen Grasflächen umgeben von hundertjährigen Bäumen dominiert, mit einem kleinen, mit Seerosen gefüllten See als Höhepunkt. Im oberen Gartenteil befindet sich der Französische Garten, der oft als ‹Mini-Versailles› bezeichnet wird, der aber ebenso Elemente der niederländischen und italienischen Gartentradition wie auch des französischen Barock zeigt. Der nahe gelegene moderne Garten mit mehrjährigen Pflanzen von ProSpecieRara bringt den Mix der Gartenstile auf den neuesten Stand.

Roger Federer, le joueur de tennis favori de Bâle, ville dont il est originaire, a choisi cette beauté à l'allure baroque pour son mariage en 2009. Il ne fait toutefois pas seulement office de terrain de jeu pour les personnes riches et discrètes de la ville : c'est aussi un fabuleux mélange de différents styles de jardin ouvert au public. La partie inférieure est composée de pelouses verdoyantes et d'imposants arbres centenaires, aboutissant à un petit lac rempli de nénuphars. Plus haut, vous trouverez le jardin français souvent appelé « mini-Versailles », bien qu'il soit tout autant inspiré des traditions de jardin hollandaise et italienne que du style classique français. Le jardin de plantes vivaces, fournies par ProSpecieRara, apporte une touche de modernité à ce mélange de styles.

ADDRESS: Bettingerstrasse 121, 4125 Riehen

TRANSPORT: Riehen, Wenkenhof, 32, 42 N22

VISITOR INFORMATION: The park is free to visit all day, the French garden is open Mon–Fri 8–17, Sunday 11–17, Saturday closed

HIGHLIGHTS: The ProSpecieRara perennial planting in the French garden looks fantastic from May onwards.

PROSPECIERARA

The ProSpecieRara foundation was created in 1982, and their mission is to save the biological diversity of rare farm animals and plant species. Similar to many of the heritage seed networks elsewhere, their methods are simple: the plant varieties must be Swiss or have been grown in Switzerland for at least 30 years to be listed in their seed inventory. If you want to have a go at growing them yourself, you can buy seedlings at one of the many seedling fairs in spring, or you can join the charity as a member and take your pick from the seed catalogue. You may recognize some of their varieties from the heritage vegetable collection on sale at the Coop; it's as good a way as any to see if you like them before growing them yourself.

Their head office is in Basel, inside the Merian Gärten (page 83) where you can find an orchard, an ornamental garden, as well as Swiss poultry breeds and Bündner Oberland sheep. The beautifully-restored building is also home to their seed bank, with row upon row of orderly boxes, full of brown envelopes of seeds. The entire affair looks more like a pharmacy than how I imagined a seed bank would look. In contrast, the garden is a real box of delights, with paths in an orderly grid pattern, allowing easy access to the lovely annuals, perennials, bulbs, fruit and vegetables.

This is not their only garden; there are six more spread across Switzerland, from the glorious perennials garden in the Wenkenpark in Riehen (page 77), to the extraordinary Erlacherhof garden in Bern, which is a baroque recreation of a garden from the 1700s.

ProSpecieRara also support 22 agricultural collections, such as the one at Schloss Wildegg, within the baroque garden and vineyards, or at ZHAW Wädenswil (page 115) as well as 3 fruit collections, in Minusio (TI) , Noflen (BE) and Riehen (BS).

For more details of all the gardens, courses, event and market, as well as the work ProSpecieRara undertake, and how you can support them, visit www.prospecierara.ch

31 ERMITAGE ARLESHEIM

How the Victorians would have loved this place! The largest and best-preserved English landscape garden in Switzerland offers grottoes, temples perched on the edges of seemingly precarious cliffs, romantic vistas and lovely dappled woods. All perfect for exciting the imagination of a well brought-up young Victorian person. The steep paths and woods are great for playing hide and seek or chasing imaginary dragons, and although the classical references of the sculptures and follies may be lost on today's visitors, it's still a great outing for several hours of exhausting playing and walking.

Wie sehr die Menschen des viktorianischen Zeitalters diesen Ort geliebt hätten! Der grösste und am besten erhaltene englische Landschaftsgarten der Schweiz bietet Grotten, Tempel am Rande von scheinbar gefährlichen Klippen, romantische Ausblicke und schöne, wie gemalte Wälder. Alles perfekt, um die Phantasie eines gebildeten jungen viktorianischen Menschen anzuregen. Die steilen Pfade und Wälder eignen sich hervorragend zum Verstecken spielen oder zum Jagen von imaginären Drachen. Und obwohl die klassischen Referenzen der Skulpturen und Prunkbauten den heutigen Besuchern nichts mehr bedeuten, ist es immer noch ein tolles Ausflugsziel, um mehrere Stunden zu spielen und spazieren zu gehen.

Ce que les Victoriens auraient aimé cet endroit ! Le jardin à l'anglaise le plus grand et le mieux entretenu de toute la Suisse présente quelques grottes, des temples perchés sur les bords de falaises à l'aspect dangereux, plusieurs vues romantiques et des bois tachetés par la lumière. Que des éléments idéaux pour stimuler l'imagination d'une jeune personne victorienne bien élevée. Les chemins escarpés et la forêt se prêtent parfaitement bien au jeu de « cache-cache » ou invitent à chasser des dragons imaginaires, et, bien que les visiteurs contemporains ne puissent peut-être plus saisir les références classiques des sculptures et des folies, cela reste un superbe lieu de sortie où passer plusieurs heures à se promener et à jouer jusqu'à épuisement.

ADDRESS: Ermitagestrasse 55, 4144 Arlesheim

TRANSPORT: Arlesheim Dorf, 15' walk

VISITOR INFORMATION: Year-round access for the park. Paths can be slippery in wet weather. Some buildings may be closed in winter.

HIGHLIGHTS: Autumn is a spectacular time to visit, as the leaves in the woods change colour and begin to fall.

Swiss Gardens Schweiz/Suisse/Switzerland

32 MERIAN GÄRTEN

Better known for their annual art fair, the lovely city of Basel also boasts a huge and glorious park on its outskirts. Originally part of the Merian family estate, it still retains the feel of a private garden, albeit a particularly large and luxurious one. The house (which now contains a restaurant) is surrounded by an English landscape park, which includes a rhododendron valley, as well as collections of bearded irises, snowdrops, clematis, peonies, fuchsias and daylilies. This is a garden that bears repeated visits; the change of the seasons brings something new every week.

Die schöne Stadt Basel, besser bekannt für ihre alljährliche Kunstmesse, verfügt auch über einen riesigen und prächtigen Park am Stadtrand. Ursprünglich Teil des Familienbesitzes der Merian Familie hat er noch immer den Charakter eines privaten Gartens, wenn auch eines besonders grossen und edlen. Das Haus, in dem sich heute ein Restaurant befindet, ist von einem englischen Landschaftspark umgeben, zu dem eine Rhododendronsenke sowie Sammlungen von Schwertlilien, Schneeglöckchen, Klematis, Pfingstrosen, Fuchsien und Tagliliengewächsen gehören. Dies ist ein Garten, der immer wieder besucht werden kann, denn der Jahreszeitenwechsel bringt jede Woche etwas Neues.

Mieux connue pour sa foire annuelle d'art contemporain, la charmante ville de Bâle peut aussi se vanter d'avoir un magnifique parc à sa périphérie. Ayant à l'origine appartenu au domaine familial Merian, il conserve l'atmosphère d'un jardin privé, bien qu'étant particulièrement grand et luxuriant. La maison qui fait à présent office de restaurant est entourée d'un parc paysager de style anglais, comprenant un vallon de rhododendrons ainsi que des collections d'iris d'Allemagne, de perce-neige, de clématites, de pivoines, de fuchsias et d'hémérocalles. Voilà un jardin qui connaît beaucoup de succès : le rythme des saisons apporte de nouvelles découvertes chaque semaine, attirant ainsi de nombreux visiteurs.

ADDRESS: Merian Gärten, Vorder Brüglingen 5, 4052 Basel

TRANSPORT: Tram 10 stop Haltestelle Neue Welt, Tram 10,11 or S-Bahn 3 Dreispitz, Tram 14 or Bus 36 St Jakob

VISITOR INFORMATION: Visiting hours are 8 to sundown, year round.

HIGHLIGHTS: Seasonal events and regular tours and talks make this a vibrant and accessible garden for all.

SWISS ORCHIDS

Switzerland is home to more than 70 wild orchid species Many of them grow readily in the wild in such places as the Swiss National Park, where the flowers are relatively easy to view. Elsewhere, there are many specific trails, like the *Orchideenlehrpfad* in Erlinsbach in the Canton of Aarau. This is managed by the AGEO, (Arbeitsgruppe Einheimische Orchideen Aargau) and allows visitors to see lots of different protected species, over a short distance, with several different biotopes, from open meadow, to dense woodland and pine forest. You can expect to see bee orchids (*Ophrys apifera*), early spider orchids (*Ophrys sphegodes*), marsh orchids (*Gymnadenia conopsea*) and helleborines (*Epipactis species*) from the middle of April. No need to take a plant book with you; there are panels along the walk about the plants, as well as QR codes, if you want to learn more about these beautiful plants.

Orchids are, like many wild flowers, under threat in Switzerland. Unscrupulous picking, which is strictly forbidden, or even plant stealing, is not unknown, and the rarest forms are often kept hidden from the public, with their locations known only to botanical specialists. The Lady's Slipper orchid, *Cypripedium calceolus*, is critically endangered in Switzerland. A so-far successful attempt has been made, to reintroduce them to the Chilpen Nature Reserve, near Diegten in Baselland, as well as 43 other locations across Switzerland. Let's hope they survive, as they are among the most impressive of the native orchids, with an inflated pouch on the flower, which looks like a shoe.

You can also enjoy native orchids without leaving your balcony or garden, as many species adapt well to home gardens. The Lady's Slipper mentioned above will grow happily in a shady spot in a regular garden with well-drained soil. They will tolerate some morning sunshine, so underneath a shrub is ideal, or in dappled shade from a tree, or on a north-facing balcony. You can buy them in good garden centres and from specialists from spring onwards. How about a nice northern marsh orchid *Dactylorhiza purpurella* or a helleborine *Epipactis palustris* to surprise the neighbours?

33 HUBER ROSEN UND PFLANZENCENTER

A waft of apple here, a hint of lemon there, and we are transported. Smell has the most extraordinary effect on us, sending us to another time or another place. Huber specialise in incredibly fragrant blooms, and a trip around their rose garden is a voyage for the nose. It's also a visual treat, with scrambling roses in the upper branches of large trees, or climbing roses elegantly draped over garden arches. The squares of well-labelled shrub roses are paint-box perfect. An ideal summery visit from May to August, and after a visit to the shop, you can take home your new favourites.

Ein Duft von Apfel hier, ein Hauch von Zitrone dort, und wir werden davongetragen. Düfte haben eine aussergewöhnliche Wirkung auf uns, da sie uns in eine andere Zeit oder an einen anderen Ort entschweben lassen. Huber ist auf hochgradig duftende Blüten spezialisiert und eine Runde durch seinen Rosengarten ist eine Reise für die Nase. Es ist auch ein optischer Leckerbissen, mit den Feldrosen in den oberen Zweigen grosser Bäume oder mit den Kletterrosen, die elegant über Gartenbögen drapiert sind, während die Beete gut beschrifteter Strauchrosen perfekt sind für den Pinsel jedes Malers. Ein ideales sommerliches Besuchsziel von Mai bis August, und nach einem Zwischenstopp im Shop kann man seine neuen Favoriten mit nach Hause nehmen.

Un arôme de pomme par-ci, un parfum de citron par-là – cela nous suffit à voyager. L'odorat a un effet des plus extraordinaires, nous propulsant dans d'autres mondes, nous renvoyant à d'autres temps. Huber est spécialisé dans les fleurs incroyablement parfumées, ce qui rend une excursion au sein de leur jardin de roses un véritable plaisir olfactif. Les yeux en profitent tout autant : des rosiers grimpants habillent les branches supérieures de grands arbres et recouvrent des arches de jardin avec élégance, et les rosiers arbustifs, décorés d'écriteaux, sont magnifiquement colorés. Une visite estivale idéale de mai à août qui, après avoir fait un tour dans la boutique, vous permettra de rentrer chez vous avec vos nouvelles plantes préférées.

ADDRESS: Rotenbühlstrasse 8, 5605 Dottikon

TRANSPORT: Dottikon Sternenplatz, buses 345 and 346

VISITOR INFORMATION: Monday–Friday (open Saturday from March–October) closed at lunchtime

HIGHLIGHTS: A magnificent rose garden and nursery, the best time to visit is in the summer during flowering season.

34 LUZERNER GARTEN

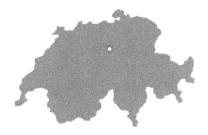

Thousands and thousands of bulbs are planted in the show garden here every year, with each year offering new flowering combinations and varieties to enjoy. The tulip is the king of the bulbs; they appear in every colour imaginable, and sometimes mixing with other spring bulbs like daffodils and irises. This mixture is complemented by the beautifully-maintained perennials, shrubs and trees that give the bulbs plenty of supportive structure. The Tulpenschau is hugely popular with local families, particularly around Mother's Day, so if you want to eat in the restaurant, book ahead. The company also specialises in orchids, and host a large show devoted to these delicate beauties every January.

Im Schaugarten werden hier jedes Jahr Abertausende von Blumenzwiebeln gepflanzt, wobei es jedes Jahr neue blühende Kombinationen und Sorten gibt. Die Tulpe ist die Königin der Zwiebelgewächse. Es gibt sie in jeder erdenklichen Farbe und sie vermischt sich sogar mit anderen Zwiebelgewächsen, wie z. B. Narzissen oder Iris. Tulpen sehen auch toll aus neben wunderschön gepflegten anderen Pflanzen – Sträuchern und Bäumen, die den Zwiebelgewächsen Halt verleihen. Die Tulpenschau ist bei einheimischen Familien sehr beliebt, insbesondere um Muttertag herum. Wenn man dann im Restaurant essen möchte, sollte man im Voraus reservieren. Das Unternehmen ist auch auf Orchideen spezialisiert und veranstaltet jedes Jahr im Januar eine grosse Show, die diesen zarten Schönheiten gewidmet ist.

Des centaines de milliers de bulbes sont plantés dans le jardin d'exposition tous les ans, donnant à chaque fois le jour à de nouvelles combinaisons et variétés. La tulipe est la reine des bulbes : elles sortent de la terre habillées de toutes les couleurs imaginables, accompagnées d'autres bulbes printaniers comme des jonquilles, des iris et des fleurs vivaces superbement entretenues – les arbres et les arbustes environnants leur offrant la structure nécessaire à leur épanouissement. La Tulpenschau est très populaire auprès des familles, surtout à la fête des mères, donc, si vous voulez aller au restaurant, pensez à réserver à l'avance. L'entreprise est également spécialisée dans les orchidées et, tous les ans au mois de janvier, elle accueille une grande exposition dédiée à ces délicates merveilles

ADDRESS: Adligenswilerstrasse 113, 6030 Ebikon

TRANSPORT: Adligenswil, Stuben bus 26

VISITOR INFORMATION: Opening hours Mo–Fr 9–18, Saturday 9–16

HIGHLIGHTS: The garden centre has several events over the year, but the most popular is the tulip show when the show garden burns bright with thousands of spring-flowering bulbs.

35 SCHLOSS HEIDEGG

If you were to create the perfect Swiss castle, what would you include? Vineyards? Woodland? Rose garden? View onto a lake? Schloss Heidegg has them all, and the view onto Lake Baldegg is worth the visit all by itself. We have the former German Chancellor Adenauer to thank for the glorious formal rose garden on the upper terrace. He visited in 1951 and said of the then-kitchen garden, "There should be roses growing here!" The plants clearly couldn't be happier being planted here, and seeing them in such great health and with so many blooms certainly makes the visitors happy too. Make sure to include a walk in the parkland on your visit: the cathedral clearing in the woods is breath-taking.

Wenn man das perfekte Schweizer Schloss konzipieren müsste, was würde das umfassen? Weinberge? Wälder? Rosengarten? Blick auf einen See? Schloss Heidegg hat all das und der Blick auf den Baldegger See ist allein schon den Besuch wert. Dem ehemaligen Bundeskanzler Adenauer haben wir den prächtigen architektonischen Rosengarten auf der oberen Terrasse zu verdanken. Er kam 1951 zu Besuch und sagte über den damaligen Küchengarten: «Hier sollten Rosen wachsen!» Die Pflanzen könnten eindeutig nicht glücklicher darüber sein, hier gepflanzt zu werden, und sie in so guter Gesundheit und mit so vielen Blüten zu sehen, macht auch die Besucher glücklich. Man sollte bei seinem Besuch einen Spaziergang im Park einplanen, denn die Lichtung inmitten des Waldes ist atemberaubend schön.

Si vous deviez créer le château suisse parfait, qu'incluriez-vous ? Des vignobles ? Des bois ? Une vue donnant sur un lac ? Le château de Heidegg possède toutes ces caractéristiques, et rien que la vue sur le lac de Baldegg vaut amplement le détour. Il faut remercier l'ancien chancelier allemand Adenauer pour le somptueux jardin classique de roses sur la terrasse supérieure. Il se rendit au château en 1951 et, en voyant les potagers de l'époque, s'exclama « On devrait faire pousser des roses ici ! ». Les plantes ne pouvaient rêver mieux que d'être placées ici, et elles ne manquent pas de ravir les visiteurs qui les voient vigoureuses et ornées de fleurs à profusion. Surtout, n'oubliez pas de vous promener dans le parc boisé lors de votre visite, car la clairière située au milieu des bois est à couper le souffle.

ADDRESS: Schloss Heidegg, Heidegg 1, 6284 Gelfingen

TRANSPORT: Gelfingen train station and then a steep walk up the hill

VISITOR INFORMATION: The park is free to visit all year, the rose garden is open April to October and costs 2CHF for adults, free with museum entry.

HIGHLIGHTS: A stunning rose garden, large woodland and beautiful views all make up the experience that is Schloss Heidegg.

GERANIUMS

What decorates every chalet and window ledge in summer? A box of geraniums, of course! Although they are not actually, botanically, called geraniums, but pelargoniums (the mix up is an ancient one), they are the most popular plant for window boxes and summer plantings in Switzerland. The addition of geraniums is relatively recent; the photographs from the "Swiss Village" created for the 1896 Exhibition in Geneva, show some window boxes on the buildings, but not the cascades of colour we know and love today.

Geraniums are often treated as annuals here in Switzerland, but are in fact perennials. They are not frost-hardy, so they need to be brought indoors for overwintering before the cold weather sets in. You can keep them in a light frost-free place, with occasional watering, until the weather warms up again in spring. Wait until the Ice Saints Days, the 11th, 12th, and 13th of May, which are traditionally the last days there could be frost, and then you can pot them up again outside.

In 1950 the city of Bern hosted a geranium event, giving away some 8000 geraniums to decorate private balconies and window boxes. It was so popular that the GeraniumMärit was created in 1957 and continues today, a two-day geranium extravaganza at the end of April.

The 1947 variety called "Stadt Bern" is still very popular, with small dark-green leaves and a rich, deep red colour. Like many of the older varieties, it flowers later, but develops into a sturdy and bushy plant by the end of the season. ProSpecie-Rara, (see page 78) the Swiss charity that promote heritage varieties of plants as well as animals, have a superb collection of older Swiss varieties. You'll find gems like "Stadt Bern" as well as rare forms like the 1906 introduction "Kardinal" with magenta flowers or "Appleblossom Rosebud" which was Queen Victoria's favourite.

You can see geraniums all over the country, not just in Bern. The small village of Grimentz, in the Val d'Anniviers, has so many of them that the tourist office have opened a Geranium Walk, where you can enjoy some of the fragrant forms. You are also unusually, encouraged to touch the leaves to release the various smells like mint, orange, pineapple and ginger. The Jardin des Senteurs in Neuchatel, as well as the Botanical Garden in Fribourg (page 37) also have large collections of these fragrant varieties.

So why is this non winter-hardy South African native so popular here? The head of the Bern garden vocational school, Lukas Zurbuchen, thinks it is the colour, which goes so well with the colour of the weathered wooden buildings in the mountains and countryside, as well as the stone buildings in Bern. I wonder, however, whether it is the reliability and the resilience of the plants, and the nod to thriftiness that appeals, as well as their glorious colours.

36 ALTER BOTANISCHER GARTEN

Tucked away in the smart banking and art gallery quarter of Zurich, there is an earlier version of the Botanical Garden, founded in 1837. Go in through the gates and up the steps and you'll find an unusual view of the city, over the Schanzengraben moat and Bauschänzli bastion – part of the Baroque fortifications of the city. The medieval herb garden at the heart is a memorial to the remarkable Zurich botanist, Conrad Gessner. The Arboretum below provides much-needed shade for lunchtime picnickers, and the 1851 glasshouse lends shelter in summer on rainy days.

Versteckt im schicken Banken- und Kunstgalerieviertel von Zürich befindet sich eine ältere Version des Botanischen Gartens, angelegt im Jahre 1837. Geht man durch die Tore und die Treppe hinauf, eröffnet sich ein ungewöhnlicher Blick auf die Stadt, über den Schanzengraben und die Bastion Bauschänzli – Teil der barocken Festungsanlagen der Stadt. Der mittelalterliche Kräutergarten im Herzen ist ein Denkmal für den bemerkenswerten Zürcher Botaniker Conrad Gessner. Das Arboretum darunter spendet Menschen dringend benötigten Schatten, in dem man es sich in der Mittagspause mit einem Picknick gut gehen lassen kann, und das Gewächshaus von 1851 bietet an sommerlichen Regentagen Schutz.

Il existe une ancienne version du jardin botanique, fondée en 1837, nichée dans le quartier chic des banques et des galeries d'art de Zurich. Franchissez le portail, montez les escaliers et vous aurez droit à une vue extraordinaire donnant sur la ville, allant du fossé Schanzengraben jusqu'au bastion Bauschänzli, faisant tous deux partie des fortifications baroques de la ville. Le jardin médiéval d'herbes aromatiques est en réalité un mémorial dédié au remarquable botaniste zurichois Conrad Gessner. L'arboretum, se situant plus bas, offre de l'ombre dont profitent les personnes venant y casser la croûte entre midi et deux, et la serre datant de 1851 sert de refuge lors des jours de pluie estivaux.

ADDRESS: Pelikanstrasse 40, 8001 Zürich

TRANSPORT: Bahnhof Selnau 8, 13,17 or Sihlstrasse 2,9, 66

VISITOR INFORMATION: The garden is free to visit all year, opening hours March to September 7–19, October–February 8–18.

HIGHLIGHTS: The Gessner garden is at the top of the garden. Stop to admire the glasshouse on the way.

37 BELVOIR PARK

The Belvoir garden was rescued from urban development by a group of concerned citizens in 1891, and is now owned by the city of Zurich. It has undergone many transformations since its first appearance as a private garden in the 1820s, which is fitting for a garden reigned over by Iris, the goddess of the rainbow. The iris season kicks off with the early-flowering *Iris reticulata* – tiny, delicate and a welcome hint that spring is on the way. Taller bearded irises follow in May with hundreds of other spring bulbs, and, in combination with the magnificent wisteria tunnel, there is plenty to enjoy well into the summer.

Der Belvoir Garten wurde 1891 von einer Gruppe engagierter Bürger vor städtebaulichen Massnahmen gerettet und befindet sich heute im Besitz der Stadt Zürich. Seit seiner Erstgestaltung als privater Garten in den 1820er Jahren hat es hier viele Veränderungen gegeben. Sehr passend für einen Garten, der von Iris, der Göttin des Regenbogens, regiert wird. Die Irissaison beginnt mit der früh blühenden *Iris reticulata*: winzig, zart und ein willkommener Hinweis darauf, dass der Frühling im Anmarsch ist. Grössere Schwertlilien folgen im Mai mit Hunderten anderer Zwiebelgewächsen des Frühlings. In Kombination mit dem prächtigen Blauregentunnel gibt es bis weit in den Sommer hinein viel zu sehen.

En 1891, un groupe de citoyens inquiets sauva le parc Belvoir du développement urbain dont il aurait autrement été victime – à présent, il appartient à la ville de Zurich. Depuis les années 1820, époque durant laquelle il fut initialement un jardin privé, il a connu un grand nombre de transformations, ce qui correspond particulièrement bien à un jardin rempli d'iris, la déesse de l'arc-en-ciel. La floraison des iris débute avec les *Iris reticulata*, les plus précoces : de nature délicate et de petite taille, ces fleurs annoncent l'arrivée du printemps tant attendu. En mai, place aux iris d'Allemagne, plus grands et accompagnés de milliers d'autres bulbes printaniers – avec le splendide tunnel de glycines, il y a largement de quoi enchanter le regard jusqu'à la période estivale.

ADDRESS: Alfred-Escher-Strasse, Mythenquai, Seestrasse, Zurich 8002

TRANSPORT: Tram 5, 6, 7, 8, 13 also buses 161, 165 Brunaustrasse, also buses 161, 165, N15 stop Sukkulenten-Sammlung

VISITOR INFORMATION: The park is open all day, every day.

HIGHLIGHTS: The floral fireworks are in April and May when the spring flowering bulbs, and the irises and the wisteria are in bloom.

Swiss Gardens Schweiz/Suisse/Switzerland

38 BOTANISCHER GARTEN ZÜRICH

Dominated by the three glass-house domes – looking like UFOs fallen to earth – the Botanical Garden is a modern, thriving garden used for teaching, research, and preservation of unique Swiss flora. The garden is in fact, the "new" botanical garden, and it moved here to the Schönau Park in 1977. The designers of the garden tried to keep as many of the old and important trees and landscape features as possible, and, as a result, the garden is an attractive blend of old and new. Modern educational gardens themed around diverse subjects like Chinese medicine or crops used in Switzerland happily rub shoulders with venerable trees and rolling lawns.

Dominiert von den drei Glas-hauskuppeln – sie sehen aus wie abgestürzte UFOs – ist der Botanische Garten ein moderner, florierender Garten, der für den Lehrbetrieb, die Forschung und Erhaltung der einzigartigen Schweizer Flora genutzt wird. Der Garten ist eigentlich der ‹neue› botanische Garten, und ist 1977 hierher in den Schönau Park umgezogen. Die Designer des Gartens versuchten, so viele der alten und wichtigen Bäume sowie so viele Landschaftselemente wie möglich zu erhalten, sodass der Garten eine attraktive Mischung aus Alt und Neu ist. Moderne Lehrgärten, die sich mit verschiedenen Themen wie der chinesischen Medizin oder den in der Schweiz gebrauchten Feldfrüchten befassen, findet man hier Seite an Seite mit ehrwürdigen Bäumen und ausgedehnten Rasenflächen.

Le jardin botanique de Zurich, sur lequel règnent les trois dômes de ses serres semblables à des soucoupes volantes, est un jardin moderne et resplendissant utilisé pour l'enseignement, la recherche et la préservation de la flore suisse. En réalité, il s'agit du « nouveau » jardin botanique qui fut aménagé dans le Schönau Park en 1977. Dans le souci de garder le plus grand nombre possible d'arbres et d'éléments essentiels qui faisaient partie de l'aménagement de l'ancien jardin, les créateurs ont composé un mélange unique et charmant de neuf et d'ancien. Des jardins modernes et éducatifs dédiés à divers thèmes, comme la médecine chinoise ou les plantes cultivées en Suisse, côtoient de nobles arbres et des pelouses verdoyantes.

ADDRESS: Botanic Garden of the University of Zurich, Zollikerstrasse 107, 8008 Zürich

TRANSPORT: Bus 33, 77 Botanischer Garten stop

VISITOR INFORMATION: The garden is free to visit all year. Opening hours March–September Mon-Fri 7–19, Sat–Sun 8–18. Winter hours slightly shorter.

HIGHLIGHTS: The giant biodomes are magnificent, inside and out.
Go from the tropics to arid desert in a few short steps!

39 CHINAGARTEN

Often cited as one of the most important Chinese gardens in Europe, the Chinagarten is a peaceful surprise in the Blatterwiese Park. You can peek in through the windows in the walls to get a taste, but I would suggest paying the small entrance fee and go in for the full banquet. The city of Kunming, in western China, gave the garden to the city of Zurich in grateful thanks for their help with the Kunming water project. The balance between the brightly coloured buildings, the lake and the trees is perfectly harmonious. The "Three Friends in Winter" – pine, bamboo and plum – are important in Chinese gardens and the specimens chosen here are beautiful.

Der Chinagarten, der oft als einer der wichtigsten chinesischen Gärten Europas bezeichnet wird, überrascht mit seinem friedlichen Ambiente im Blatterwiese Park. Für einen Vorgeschmack kann man durch die Mauerfenster hineinschauen, aber es empfiehlt sich, den geringen Eintrittspreis zu zahlen und seinen Gartenbesuch so richtig auszukosten. Die Stadt Kunming in Westchina hat der Stadt Zürich den Garten als Dankeschön für ihre Hilfe beim Wasserprojekt Kunming geschenkt. Das Gleichgewicht zwischen den bunten Gebäuden, dem See und den Bäumen ist perfekt harmonisch. Die ‹drei Freunde im Winter› – Kiefer, Bambus und Pflaume – sind wichtig in chinesischen Gärten und die hier zu bewundernden Exemplare sind einfach nur wunderschön.

Souvent considéré comme l'un des jardins chinois les plus importants d'Europe, le Chinagarten est une agréable surprise au sein du Blatterwiese Park. Vous pouvez le contempler à travers les fenêtres de la paroi, mais je vous conseille de vous procurer un billet d'entrée au coût peu onéreux pour pouvoir pleinement profiter de sa beauté paisible. La ville de Kunming, en Chine occidentale, a offert ce jardin à Zurich pour la remercier de son aide apportée au projet d'approvisionnement en eau. L'équilibre, qui a été trouvé entre les bâtiments de couleurs vives, le lac et les arbres, produit un effet des plus harmonieux. Le thème des « trois amis de l'hiver » – représentés par le pin, le bambou et le cerisier – est essentiel dans les jardins chinois et les variétés choisies ici sont splendides.

ADDRESS: Bellerivestrasse 138, 8008 Zurich

TRANSPORT: Bus 916, 912 stop Chinagarten

VISITOR INFORMATION: Opening hours 11–19 from mid March to mid October. There is small entry fee for adults and children aged 5 to 16.

HIGHLIGHTS: Fresh from the 2018 renovations, the buildings that help make this garden so special will be gleaming for visitors from 2019.

Swiss Gardens Schweiz/Suisse/Switzerland

40 FIFA GARDEN

How do you travel round the world without leaving Zurich? Simple. Come to the FIFA garden. Each part of the garden represents one of the six footballing continents, with typical plants from the region. Giant trees for South America, Everglades-inspired mosses and ferns for North America, and wide-open grassy spaces for the African savannah. The garden is brought together by repeated plantings of grasses and grouped trees. Thousands of spring flowering bulbs light up the grassy areas from February onwards. The boundary is planted with native trees and shrubs that blend seamlessly into the woodland beyond, making the garden feel much larger than it is.

Wie kann man um die Welt reisen, ohne Zürich zu verlassen? Ganz einfach. Man besucht den FIFA-Garten. Jeder Teil des Gartens stellt einen der sechs Fussball-Kontinente dar, mit typischen Pflanzen aus der Region. Riesige Bäume für Südamerika, von den Everglades inspirierte Moose und Farne für Nordamerika und weitläufige Grasflächen für die afrikanische Savanne. Der Garten wird durch wiederholte Anpflanzungen von Gräsern und gruppierten Bäumen zusammengeführt. Tausende von Zwiebelgewächsen lassen ab Februar die Grasflächen erblühen. Das Grundstück ist durch einheimische Bäume und Sträucher abgegrenzt, die nahtlos in den Wald dahinter übergehen, sodass sich der Garten viel grösser anfühlt als er ist.

Comment faire le tour du monde sans quitter Zurich ? Facile : allez au jardin de la FIFA. Chaque partie représente l'un des six continents footballistiques, toutes décorées de plantes typiques de ces régions. Des arbres gigantesques pour l'Amérique du Sud, de la mousse et des fougères inspirées des Everglades pour l'Amérique du Nord et de grands espaces ouverts rappelant la savane africaine. Les diverses zones sont liées entre elles par du gazon et des arbres plantés en groupes. Des milliers de bulbes à fleurs ornent les pelouses à partir de février. Les limites du jardin sont habillées d'arbres et d'arbustes indigènes qui se mêlent harmonieusement aux bois se trouvant plus loin, donnant l'impression que le jardin est bien plus grand qu'il ne l'est en réalité.

ADDRESS: FIFA-Strasse 20, 8044 Zürich

TRANSPORT: Zoo, tram 5,6, bus N17, plus a short walk

VISITOR INFORMATION: Free to visit all day, every day. It belongs to the offices of FIFA, where there are people working, so please behave appropriately.

HIGHLIGHTS: The garden is designed so that there is something to enjoy in every month, from the spring flowering bulbs to the ornamental grasses in late summer.

41 KLUS PARK

Can a garden be made of love? If the Klus Park garden – which surrounds a retirement home in a quiet suburb of Zurich – is any indication, then yes. The large trees structure the garden, with gentle paths that wind between them and lead from the house into the garden and to the pond, the restaurant and the terrace, as well as to the work areas where residents can plant and enjoy the outdoors. The garden is well cared for with imaginative container planting and flowerbeds that change regularly. Enjoy the game of "spot the heart", in the flowerbeds, in the garlands on the doors and hanging from available trees.

Kann ein Garten aus Liebe gemacht werden? Wenn der Garten des Klus Parks – der ein Seniorenheim in einem ruhigen Vorort von Zürich umgibt – ein Hinweis ist, dann ja. Die grossen Bäume strukturieren den Garten mit leichten Wegen, die sich zwischen ihnen schlängeln und vom Haus in den Garten und zum Teich, zum Restaurant und zur Terrasse sowie zu den Arbeitsbereichen führen, wo die Bewohner den Outdoorbereich bepflanzen und geniessen können. Der Garten ist gut gepflegt mit seinen phantasievollen Kübelpflanzen sowie regelmässig veränderten Blumenbeeten. Erfreuen Sie sich an dem Spiel ‹Finden Sie das Herz› in den Blumenbeeten, in den Girlanden an den Türen und herunterbaumelnd von den vorhandenen Bäumen.

Un jardin peut-il être fait d'amour ? Si on se fie à celui de Klus Park, entourant une maison de retraite dans une banlieue calme de Zurich, alors la réponse à cette question est oui. Les grands arbres structurent le jardin, agrémenté de sentiers passant à travers les végétations. Depuis la maison, ces chemins vous conduisent au jardin puis à l'étang, au restaurant et à la terrasse ainsi qu'aux aires de travail où les résidents peuvent s'adonner à des activités de plantation et profiter de l'air frais. Le jardin est bien entretenu avec des bacs ingénieux pour les plantes et des parterres qui changent régulièrement d'allure. Amusez-vous à « trouver les cœurs » déposés dans les plates-bandes et sur les guirlandes accrochées aux portes et aux arbres.

ADDRESS: Asylstrasse 130, 8032 Zürich

TRANSPORT: Bus Klusplatz 31,33 tram 8,9

VISITOR INFORMATION: The garden is free to visit all day, every day.

HIGHLIGHTS: High summer is fabulous when the borders are buzzing with bees, but this garden also has a special charm in winter with snow on the ground.

42 MFO PARK

Imagine a spider's web covering an old industrial building. Now take away the building and leave the spider's web, and you have the structure for the MFO Park. The metal webbing represents the shape and space of the former printing works and provides a structure for climbing plants that are progressively clothing the walls. The "Park-Haus" building is on several levels, giving different perspectives on the planting around and inside the garden, down to the sparkly recycled glass floor. Benches on the upper level are popular for picnics, with leafy views outside to the post-industrial backdrop, the newly planted trees and the sky.

Stellen Sie sich ein Spinnennetz vor, das ein altes Industriegebäude bedeckt. Jetzt denkt man sich das Gebäude weg, und schon hat man die Struktur des MFO-Parks. Das Metallgerüst repräsentiert die Form und den Raum der ehemaligen Druckerei vor Ort und bietet eine Struktur für Kletterpflanzen, die nach und nach die Wände auskleiden. Das ‹Park-Haus› ist mehrstöckig und eröffnet unterschiedliche Perspektiven auf die Bepflanzung rund um und innerhalb des Gartens sowie herunter zum funkelnden recycelten Glasboden. Bänke auf der oberen Ebene sind beliebt für Picknicks, mit einem grünen Blick auf die postindustrielle Kulisse, die neu gepflanzten Bäume und den Himmel.

Imaginez une toile d'araignée recouvrant un vieux bâtiment industriel. À présent, gommez le bâtiment de votre imagination tout en laissant la toile d'araignée : voilà à quoi ressemble la structure du MFO Park. La toile en métal représente la forme et la surface de l'ancienne imprimerie, et elle offre une structure solide pour les diverses plantes grimpantes qui l'habillent de plus en plus au fil du temps. Nommé « Park-Haus », le bâtiment présente plusieurs étages, offrant ainsi différentes vues sur les plantations autour et à l'intérieur du jardin, jusqu'au sol en verre recyclé qui scintille à la lumière. Au niveau supérieur, les bancs ont la cote auprès des visiteurs pour des pique-niques entourés d'un panorama mêlant des arbres récemment plantés, le ciel et un arrière-plan post-industriel.

ADDRESS: James Joyce Strasse, 8050 Zürich

TRANSPORT: Train Zurich Oerlikon, bus Bahnhof Oerlikon Nord 80, N7, plus a short walk

VISITOR INFORMATION: The MFO Park is free to visit all day, every day.

HIGHLIGHTS: This remarkable green space will turn your ideas upside down of what a park should be, all while providing a living laboratory for climbing plants on the outside.

43 PALAIS RECHBERG

The Rechberg Palace is one of the most important and beautiful baroque buildings in Zurich, and the gardens that surround it are just as lovely. The house and gardens have been rebuilt and renovated over the centuries. The famous Swiss landscape architecture firm, Hager Partner, designed a new interpretation that combines the traditional baroque lower garden – planted with seasonal bedding – with a very modern terraced upper garden. The upper garden is dominated by dark green clipped yew cones, modern benches and strips of lawn, perfect for perching on to peek over the rooftops to the Uetliberg beyond.

Das Stadtpalais Rechberg ist eines der bedeutendsten und schönsten Barockgebäude Zürichs, und die umliegenden Gärten sind ebenso schön. Das Haus und die Gärten wurden im Laufe der Jahrhunderte wieder aufgebaut und renoviert. Das renommierte Schweizer Landschaftsarchitekturbüro Hager Partner entwarf eine neue Interpretation, die den traditionellen unteren Barockgarten – bepflanzt mit saisonalen Gartenpflanzen – mit einem sehr modernen terrassierten oberen Garten verbindet. Der obere Garten wird dominiert von dunkelgrün gestutzten Eibenkegeln, modernen Sitzmöglichkeiten und Rasenstreifen, die sich perfekt als gemütliches Plätzchen eignen, um den Blick über die Dächer zum Uetliberg zu geniessen.

Le Palais Rechberg est l'un des édifices baroques les plus importants et les plus beaux de Zurich, et les jardins qui l'entourent sont tout aussi charmants. À travers les siècles, le bâtiment et les jardins ont été reconstruits et rénovés à maintes reprises. La célèbre entreprise de paysagisme, Hager Partner, a conçu un nouvel aménagement qui se traduit par une combinaison du jardin traditionnel inférieur de style baroque – décoré de parterres saisonniers – avec un jardin supérieur en terrasses à l'allure très moderne. Ce dernier, bordé d'ifs vert foncé et taillés en forme de cône, est composé de bancs contemporains ainsi que de rectangles de pelouse, vous offrant un endroit parfait pour admirer le panorama – contemplez les toits environnants et posez votre regard au-delà de l'Uetliberg.

ADDRESS: Hirschengraben 40, 8001 Zürich

TRANSPORT: Neumarkt Tram 3,11, bus 31, 31E, 33E

VISITOR INFORMATION: Opening hours
1 April–31 October: 6–21.
1 November–31 March: 8–18.
The garden is free to visit.

HIGHLIGHTS: The seasonal bedding is fabulous, particularly when the spring flowering bulbs are in bloom from March to May.

44 SELEGER MOOR

The original owner of this garden, Robert Seleger, was a keen collector and hybridiser of rhododendrons and created a magnificent garden in a peat bog. The shelter belt of trees, planted to protect the more delicate specimens from the cold winds in this region, have grown into a small forest worth visiting in its own right. Besides the rhododendrons, you can find ferns, hydrangeas, peonies and water lilies. Robert Seleger also had a great eye for garden scenes, and the bridges, trees and vistas across the garden and beyond are worthy of the best landscape painters. The excellent plant nursery will provide you with plants and advice so you can re-create your own Seleger Moor at home.

Der ursprüngliche Besitzer dieses Gartens, Robert Seleger, war ein begeisterter Sammler und Züchter von Rhododendren und erschuf einen prächtigen Garten in einem Torfmoor. Der Schutzgürtel aus Bäumen, der zum Schutz der empfindlicheren Exemplare vor den kalten Winden in dieser Region angepflanzt wurde, hat sich zu einem kleinen Wald entwickelt, der schon für sich genommen einen Besuch wert ist. Abgesehen von den Rhododendren gibt es Farne, Hortensien, Pfingstrosen und Seerosen. Robert Seleger hatte auch ein gutes Auge für Gartenszenen, und die Brücken, Bäume und Aussichten auch über den Garten hinaus sind würdiges Material für die besten Landschaftsmaler. Die grossartige Gärtnerei versorgt Sie mit Pflanzen und Ratschlägen, damit Sie Ihr eigenes Seleger Moor zu Hause gestalten können.

Le premier propriétaire de ce jardin, Robert Seleger, était un grand collectionneur de rhododendrons qu'il aimait également hybrider. Il a créé un splendide jardin au sein d'une tourbière. L'abrivent composé d'arbres, planté à l'origine afin de protéger les spécimens plus délicats des vents froids de la région, est devenu une véritable petite forêt qui vaut la peine d'être visitée. Outre les rhododendrons, vous trouverez des fougères, des hortensias, des pivoines et des nénuphars. Robert Seleger avait aussi l'œil pour les décors de jardin – ainsi, les ponts, les arbres et les différentes vues de part et d'autre du jardin sont dignes des meilleurs peintres paysagistes. Vous trouverez de quoi recréer votre propre Seleger Moor à la maison dans la superbe pépinière.

ADDRESS: Seleger-Moor-Strasse, 8911 Rifferswil

TRANSPORT: Seleger Moor, post bus

VISITOR INFORMATION: Opening hours are Monday-Saturday 8–18 from the end of March to the end of October. Price is 15CHF for adults, free for children under 15.

HIGHLIGHTS: There is something to enjoy every month in the park, as well as lots of workshops and talks.

45 SUKKULENTEN-SAMMLUNG

If you think that everything in this collection is spiny, spiky or prickly, then you'll be missing out on a huge part of what's on offer here. You'll find fluffy, fragrant and shiny specimens here too. The enormous range of cacti and succulents are well represented, with 4500 different species from 78 different plant families. They are divided up between seven greenhouses, such as the one devoted to giant plants, as well as a cold frame and a large outdoor rockery.

Wenn man glaubt, alles in dieser Sammlung sei dornig, stachelig oder stechend, dann verpasst man einen Grossteil dessen, was hier geboten wird. Hier gibt es auch flauschige, duftende und glänzende Exemplare. Die enorme Vielfalt an Kakteen und Sukkulenten ist gut vertreten, mit 4500 verschiedenen Arten aus 78 unterschiedlichen Pflanzenfamilien. Sie verteilen sich auf sieben Gewächshäuser, wie das den Riesenpflanzen gewidmete, sowie ein Frühbeet und eine grosse Steingartenanlage im Freien.

Si vous pensez que cette collection n'est faite que d'épines ou de piquants, vous risquez de passer à côté de plusieurs surprises. En effet, vous découvrirez également des spécimens parfumés, à l'aspect pelucheux ou brillant. Le très large éventail de cactus et de plantes grasses y est particulièrement bien représenté, exposant ainsi 4500 variétés de 78 familles de plantes différentes. Elles sont réparties dans sept serres, comme celle dédiée aux plantes géantes, ainsi que dans un châssis froid ; d'autres encore sont dispersées dans une grande rocaille à l'extérieur.

ADDRESS: Mythenquai 88, 8002 Zürich

TRANSPORT: Sukkulentensammlung tram 7, bus 161, 165

VISITOR INFORMATION: Opening hours 9–16:30 every day, all year including Sundays and Bank Holidays.

HIGHLIGHTS: You'll find free tours, additional focus topic exhibits, weekly advice sessions and even a night time visit for the rare occasions when the Queen of the Night cactus is in bloom

46 ZHAW WÄDENSWIL

This garden is best known locally for the sumptuous peony garden, with more than 250 different varieties on show. But it would be a pity to visit this garden only in spring, as there is plenty to enjoy in summer and early autumn too. Regular changes to the planting created by the students and gardeners, as well as lovely views down to the lake, combine to make this a garden that repays the effort to get here many times over. The mixed perennial plantings, where the school trials plant mixes for public and private gardens, are lovely all year round, and inspirational for anyone looking to make a change to their own planting.

Dieser Garten ist im Umkreis für den üppigen Pfingstrosengarten mit mehr als 250 verschiedenen Sorten bekannt. Aber es wäre schade, diesen Garten nur im Frühjahr zu besuchen, da es hier auch im Sommer und Frühherbst viel zu bestaunen gibt. Regelmässige Änderungen an der von den Studenten und Gärtnern angelegten Bepflanzung sowie schöne Ausblicke hinunter auf den See entschädigen um ein Vielfaches für den Aufwand, hierher zu kommen. Die gemischten mehrjährigen Anpflanzungen, mit denen die Schule Pflanzenmischungen für öffentliche und private Gärten ausprobiert, sind das ganze Jahr über schön und inspirierend für jeden, der seine eigene Bepflanzung verändern möchte.

Ce jardin est surtout connu dans le coin pour son somptueux jardin de pivoines, présentant plus de 250 variétés différentes. Mais il serait dommage de le visiter uniquement au printemps, en raison de toutes les choses qu'il y a aussi à voir en été et au début de l'automne. Il vaut largement le coup de s'y rendre plusieurs fois, notamment à cause des changements réguliers apportés à l'agencement des plantes créé par les étudiants et les jardiniers, et aussi pour ses vues magnifiques donnant sur le lac. Les mélanges de plantes vivaces, plantés par les étudiants en tant qu'expérimentations pour des jardins publics et privés, sont non seulement d'une grande beauté tout au long de l'année, mais aussi une source d'inspiration pour ceux qui aimeraient apporter un souffle nouveau à leur jardin.

ADDRESS: Grüentalstrasse 14, 8820 Wädenswil

TRANSPORT: Campus Grüental, bus 123, 126, 150 plus a short walk through the campus

VISITOR INFORMATION: Opening hours are during the hours of daylight, all year round. There is no charge to visit the garden.

HIGHLIGHTS: Peonies, prairie planting, and lots of inventive new mini gardens created by the students, this is a busy and ever-changing garden.

URBAN GARDENING

Gardens in cities can have huge benefits for both city-dwellers and the gardeners themselves; they provide food, space for recreation, and foster the integration of people from different backgrounds, forming social networks and improving physical and mental health. In Switzerland, allotment gardening has long been a popular way to bring a piece of the countryside – wherever you're from – to the city. The first examples of allotment gardens in Geneva date back to the 14th century and are on top of the ramparts of the old town. The arrival of two waves of Huguenots to the area, from 1570 and after the revocation of the Edict of Nantes in 1685, saw an increase in small-scale gardens and market gardening around the Plainpalais area, near the Arve river. These Huguenot arrivals introduced some new varieties which became some of the oldest and most popular regional vegetables. The cardoon, like a giant thistle, under the name "Epineux argenté de Plainpalais" can still be seen growing in the fields in the canton, as well as in the walled vegetable garden at the Château de Prangins (page 21). It's an enormous plant, growing up to 2m tall, and the production methods have barely changed since their mention in the *Encylopédie d'Yverdon* published in the 1770s. The plants are bound up with string in October, using a special tool, the *pince à cardon* to avoid getting prickled by the fearsome spines on the stems. The plants are then wrapped in paper or jute to blanch them, and can be picked and eaten a month later. The stems are stripped of prickles, cooked in water or milk and then topped with a béchamel sauce.

If you would like to grow your own, then maybe an allotment is for you. For serious gardeners who want a reasonable plot and are prepared to spend several hours per week gardening, the Swiss Federation of Allotment Gardeners (*Fédération suisse des jardins familiaux* or *Schweizer Familien-gärtner-Verband*) has 23,000 members across the country. They provide information and support for their members as well as managing the inscriptions and the waiting lists, which can be up to two years in the most popular areas.

If you feel like this may be a bit much, there are other organisations that let you get involved in urban gardening, without the need for such a serious time investment. The Merkurgarten in Zurich, for example, allows local residents to garden and get together, for only 50 Swiss Francs per year, and the extraordinary Urban Agriculture Basel have dozens of small projects all over the city, with the intent of bringing people together to grow and share food.

47 BAUMMUSEUM ENEA

This is a special experience in Switzerland: a museum for trees. Every tree is carefully labelled with the Latin and common name, region of origin, and when it was planted. Each tree also has a particular feature, shape or size that justifies its inclusion in the collection. Cloud-pruned hedges lead the eye to the hills beyond. A limited palette of plants, hydrangeas, grasses add to – but don't distract from – the glorious specimens in the foreground. The recent addition of large-scale works of art, carefully placed among the trees, provide a contemporary counterpoint to the beauty of the natural world.

Das ist ein besonderes Erlebnis in der Schweiz: ein Museum für Bäume. Jeder Baum ist sorgfältig mit dem lateinischen und dem allgemeinen Namen, der Herkunftsregion und dem Zeitpunkt der Anpflanzung gekennzeichnet. Jeder Baum hat auch eine bestimmte Eigenschaft, Form oder Grösse, die seine Aufnahme in die Sammlung rechtfertigt. Wolkenförmig gestutzte Hecken führen das Auge zu den Hügeln dahinter. Eine begrenzte Palette von Pflanzen, Hortensien und Gräsern ergänzt die prächtigen Exemplare im Vordergrund – lenkt aber nicht davon ab. Die kürzlich hinzugekommenen grossformatigen Kunstwerke, die sorgfältig zwischen den Bäumen gepflanzt wurden, bilden einen zeitgenössischen Kontrapunkt zur Schönheit der natürlichen Welt.

Voici une expérience unique en Suisse : un musée de l'arbre. Chaque arbre a été minutieusement orné d'une étiquette comprenant son nom latin et son nom commun, sa région d'origine et la date à laquelle il a été planté. En outre, tous les arbres possèdent une caractéristique, une forme ou une taille particulière qui justifie sa raison d'être au sein de cette collection. Des haies taillées en forme de nuages invitent à poser son regard au-delà des collines. Une petite palette composée de plantes, d'hortensias et d'herbes embellit les magnifiques spécimens se trouvant au premier plan. Les œuvres d'art grand format qui y ont été récemment ajoutées, placées avec soin au milieu des arbres, offrent un jeu de contraste entre ces éléments contemporains et la beauté du monde naturel.

ADDRESS: Buechstrasse 12, 8645 Jona SG

TRANSPORT: St Dionys stop bus 621, 622, 623 or Buechstrasse West bus 621. NB St Dionys runs all day with a 1 km walk, Buechstrasse only occasionally during the day

VISITOR INFORMATION: Cost 15 CHF adults, 12 CHF students. Open Mon–Fi 9–18, Saturday 10–17, reduced hours in winter. Closed public holidays and Sundays.

HIGHLIGHTS: A whistle-stop tour of the most beautiful trees and modern art, together in a fabulous setting

48 ISOLE DI BRISSAGO

We have Antoinette de St Léger, a Russian noblewoman, to thank for the creation of this garden. At age twenty-nine – and accompanied by her third husband – she chose the larger of the two Brissago islands for her home. The underlying rock was improved by boatloads of soil and manure, and a sub-tropical paradise was created. Today the garden is divided by region, with plants perfectly chosen to thrive in this unique micro-climate. You'll find plant treasures around every corner, as well as newer, educational additions like the Magical Garden. You can only access the garden by boat, so make sure you leave plenty of time to see everything as well as enjoy the view from one of the many benches dotted around the grounds.

Die Gestaltung dieses Gartens verdanken wir Antoinette de St. Léger, einer russischen Adligen. Im Alter von 29 Jahren – in Begleitung ihres dritten Mannes! – wählte sie die grössere der beiden Brissago-Inseln als ihr Zuhause. Der darunterliegende Fels wurde durch Bootsladungen von Erde und Dung verbessert und darauf ein subtropisches Paradies erschaffen. Heute ist der Garten nach Regionen gegliedert, mit Pflanzen, die ausgewählt wurden, um in diesem einzigartigen Mikroklima zu gedeihen. Man trifft an jeder Ecke auf Pflanzenkleinode, aber auch auf neuere, lehrreiche Ergänzungen wie den Magischen Garten. Man kann den Garten nur mit dem Boot erreichen, also sollte man sich viel Zeit lassen, um alles zu erkunden und den Ausblick von einem der vielen auf dem Gelände verstreuten Bänke auskosten.

C'est à Antoinette de Saint Léger, aristocrate russe, que nous devons la création de ce jardin. À l'âge de vingt-neuf ans – et accompagnée par son troisième mari ! – elle choisit la plus grande des deux îles de Brissago pour y élire domicile. La couche de roche sous-jacente fut recouverte de cargaisons entières de bonne terre et de fumier et un véritable paradis subtropical fut créé. De nos jours, le jardin est réparti en régions, abritant des plantes choisies spécialement pour s'épanouir dans ce microclimat unique. Vous trouverez de véritables trésors végétaux ainsi que des ajouts plus récents à caractère éducatif, comme le jardin magique. On accède au jardin uniquement en bateau. Il faut donc prévoir assez de temps pour tout visiter et profiter de la vue depuis l'un des nombreux bancs.

ADDRESS: Parco botanico del Canton Ticino, 6614, Isole di Brissago

TRANSPORT: Ferry terminal Isole di Brissago

VISITOR INFORMATION: Costs 8 CHF for adults and 2.50 for children, open from March–October when the ferry is operating. Access is only possible by boat.

HIGHLIGHTS: An extraordinary collection of plants, arranged by region, and all on an island with glorious views in every direction

122

49 PARCO SAN GRATO

Where would we be without wealthy garden-makers gifting their green spaces to the nation? We have a zipper magnate, a steel mill owner, and the UBS bank to thank for this garden. The first owner created this steep playground for his friends and family to enjoy at weekends and on horseback, and the second owner cleared a lot of the native beech and chestnut woodland, and replaced it with the rhododendrons and azaleas that you can see today. More recent plant additions include new daylily and hydrangea plantings, to extend the period of interest well beyond the springtime flowering frenzy.

Was wären wir ohne wohlhabende Gartenbauern, die ihre Grünflächen der Nation schenken? Diesen Garten haben wir einem Reissverschluss-Grossindustriellen, einem Stahlwerksbesitzer und der UBS-Bank zu verdanken. Der erste Besitzer erschuf diesen steilen Spielplatz für seine Freunde und Familie, um dort auch zu Pferd die Wochenenden zu verbringen, und der zweite Besitzer fällte einen Grossteil der einheimischen Buchen- und Kastanienwälder und ersetzte ihn durch die Rhododendren und Azaleen, die man heute sehen kann. Neuere Pflanzenergänzungen umfassen neue Anpflanzungen von Taglilien und Hortensien, um den Zeitraum weit über den Blütenrausch des Frühlings hinaus interessant zu halten.

Que ferions-nous sans les riches créateurs de jardin offrant leurs espaces verts au pays ? C'est grâce au magnat d'une marque de fermetures Éclair, au propriétaire d'une sidérurgie et à la banque UBS que nous pouvons profiter de ce jardin. Le premier propriétaire créa cette aire de jeu sur la pente de la colline pour que sa famille et ses amis puissent y passer leurs week-ends à dos de cheval. Le second propriétaire, quant à lui, déboisa le terrain, abattant ainsi une forêt d'hêtres et de châtaigniers pour la remplacer par les rhododendrons et les azalées que vous pouvez voir de nos jours. Des plantations supplémentaires, comme des hémérocalles et des hortensias, complètent depuis peu le parc afin de prolonger la frénésie printanière et de pouvoir exhiber des fleurs jusqu'en été.

ADDRESS: Via San Grato, 6914 Carona

TRANSPORT: Carona, Paese

VISITOR INFORMATION: Free to visit all day, every day

HIGHLIGHTS: The big show is in spring when the rhododendrons and azaleas are in bloom, but new playgrounds, a sensory trail, well-placed artworks and inventive and fun pathways make this an excellent day out, whatever the time of year.

Swiss Gardens Schweiz/Suisse/Switzerland

50 PARCO DELLE CAMELIE

Locarno is known as *La Città delle Camelie*, "the City of the Camellia", and if you had wanted to design the perfect place for these lovely plants, you'd be hard-pressed to do better than here. With acidic soil, the highest average yearly temperature in Switzerland, less frost and more days of sunshine than neighbouring Lugano, it's no surprise that camellias do so well here. The park, opened in 2005, is open year round, and is popular with locals who come for a quiet swim or to enjoy the glorious lake views. The real fireworks are between early March and the end of April, with the Camellia Festival right in the middle.

Locarno ist bekannt als *La Città delle Camelie* (die Stadt der Kamelien) und wenn man den perfekten Ort für diese schönen Pflanzen hätte entwerfen wollen, hätte man es kaum besser machen können als hier. Mit saurem Boden, der höchsten durchschnittlichen Jahrestemperatur der Schweiz, weniger Frost und mehr Sonnentagen als im benachbarten Lugano ist es kein Wunder, dass Kamelien hier so gut gedeihen. Der 2005 eröffnete Park ist das ganze Jahr über geöffnet und bei Einheimischen beliebt, die zum Schwimmen oder zum Geniessen des herrlichen Seeblicks herkommen. Das echte Feuerwerk findet zwischen Anfang März und Ende April statt und das Kamelien Festival genau dazwischen.

Locarno est connue sous le nom de La Città delle Camelie, « la ville aux camélias », et si vous aviez dû créer l'endroit parfait pour ces jolies plantes, vous auriez eu beaucoup de mal à faire mieux. Avec son sol acide, la température moyenne la plus élevée du pays ainsi que la chance d'avoir moins de gel et plus de soleil que sa voisine Lugano, ce n'est pas surprenant que ces fleurs se portent aussi bien ici. Le parc, qui existe depuis 2005, est ouvert tout au long de l'année et connaît beaucoup de succès auprès des gens du coin qui viennent pour y piquer une tête, au calme, ou tout simplement pour profiter des magnifiques vues sur le lac. Les fleurs atteignent leur apogée entre le début du mois de mars et la fin du mois d'avril, et la Fête des Camélias tombe exactement entre ces dates.

ADDRESS: Via Gioacchino Respini 7, 6600 Locarno

TRANSPORT: Locarno Lido bus 2

VISITOR INFORMATION: Access is free except during the Camellia Festival, when it costs 5CHF. Opening times are March–September: 9–18, slightly reduced hours in winter.

HIGHLIGHTS: Springtime or autumn, there are camellias in bloom, and if you miss these periods, then there's always the lake for paddling or admiring.

Swiss Gardens Schweiz/Suisse/Switzerland

51 PARCO SCHERRER

It's hard to imagine that less than a hundred years ago this hillside was covered in vineyards and native beech and chestnut woods. Hermann Scherrer bought a hectare of land with a house, and gradually converted the existing slope and vegetation into the splendid terraces and plantings that you see today. He added statues and scaled versions of temples and grottoes to remind him of his travels. The Mediterranean areas give way to an Asian section where you will find a Siamese tea house, and Arab and Indian buildings, all paired with appropriate plantings.

Es ist schwer vorstellbar, dass dieser Hang noch vor weniger als hundert Jahren von Weinbergen und einheimischen Buchen- und Kastanienwäldern bedeckt war. Hermann Scherrer kaufte ein Hektar Land mit einem Haus und verwandelte die vorhandenen Böschungen und die Vegetation nach und nach in die prächtigen Terrassen und Bepflanzungen, die man heute hier sieht. Er fügte Statuen und skalierte Versionen von Tempeln und Grotten hinzu, um sich an seine Reisen zu erinnern. Der Mittelmeerraum geht über in einen asiatischen Teil, in dem sich ein siamesisches Teehaus sowie arabische und indische Gebäude befinden, gepaart mit entsprechenden Anpflanzungen.

Difficile de s'imaginer qu'il y a moins d'un siècle, cette colline était tapissée de vignobles ainsi que de forêts remplies de hêtres et de châtaigniers indigènes. Hermann Scherrer y acheta une maison accompagnée d'un hectare de terrain et convertit progressivement la pente et la végétation de l'époque en de splendides terrasses garnies de plantes et de fleurs. Il ajouta diverses statues, temples et grottes à échelle réduite inspirés par ses nombreux voyages. Les zones méditerranéennes mènent à la partie asiatique du parc au sein de laquelle vous trouverez une maison de thé siamoise ainsi que des édifices arabes et indiens, tous décorés de plantes typiques de ces régions.

ADDRESS: Riva di Pilastri 20, 6922 Morcote

TRANSPORT: Morcote Parco Scherrer 431 bus, or Piazza Grande 431 and 440, also boat Morcote Lago

VISITOR INFORMATION: Costs 7 CHF for adults, 2 CHF for children up to 16. Openng hours 10–17h, an hour later in high summer.

HIGHLIGHTS: There is always something in flower here, and the sculptures and views onto the lake make for a decidedly unique experience.

52 VIVAIO EISENHUT
E PARCO BOTANICO GAMBAROGNO

There aren't many nurseries or botanical gardens that would boast about how much rain and how little sunshine they get, but Eisenhut is a bit unusual. Situated on the shady side of Lago Maggiore, the plants here benefit from cooler summers and more rainfall than the rest of the region, and the vibrantly healthy plants clearly love the conditions. The current owner's father started the nursery, and encouraged by the British diplomat and botanist, Sir Peter Smithers, branched out into magnolias. The steep hillside botanic park is full of well-labelled trees and shrubs and many of the plants can then be bought in the nursery.

Es gibt nicht viele Baumschulen oder botanische Gärten, die damit prahlen würden, wie viel Regen und wie wenig Sonnenschein sie bekommen, aber Eisenhut ist da etwas ungewöhnlich. An der schattigen Seite des Lago Maggiore gelegen, profitieren die Pflanzen hier von kühleren Sommern und mehr Niederschlag als im Rest der Region, und die leuchtend bunten, gesunden Pflanzen lieben diese Bedingungen offensichtlich. Der Vater des jetzigen Besitzers gründete die Baumschule und pflanzte mit Unterstützung des britischen Diplomaten und Botanikers Sir Peter Smithers Magnolien an. Der botanische Park mit dem steil abfallenden Hang ist voller gut gekennzeichneter Bäume und Sträucher; viele der Pflanzen können in der Baumschule gekauft werden.

Rares sont les pépinières ou les jardins botaniques qui se vanteraient de recevoir beaucoup de pluie et peu de soleil, mais Eisenhut est quelque peu spéciale. Se trouvant du côté ombragé du Lago Maggiore, les plantes y jouissent de températures fraîches en été et ont la chance de profiter davantage de pluie que le reste de la région – l'aspect vigoureux des plantes témoigne clairement de leur bien-être dans ces conditions météorologiques. C'est le père du propriétaire actuel qui ouvrit la pépinière et, encouragé par le diplomate et botaniste anglais Sir Peter Smithers, commença à planter et à entretenir des magnolias. Le parc botanique sur la colline escarpée est rempli d'arbres et d'arbustes, tous ornés d'étiquettes, et vous pouvez acheter un grand nombre de ces plantes dans la pépinière.

ADDRESS: Via Parco Botanico 21, 6575 Nazarro

TRANSPORT: Piazzogna, Parco Botanico bus 326, 330

VISITOR INFORMATION: Opening hours Monday–Saturday 7:30–19, Sunday 8:30–19, winter 10–17. Nursery hours restricted in winter and high summer, check before you go. No credit cards

HIGHLIGHTS: Visit in springtime for the magnolias, azaleas and rhododendrons, or late summer for the day lilies and citrus.

RHODODENDRONS

When is a rose not a rose? When it's a rhododendron. The Swiss singer Polo Hofer sang about an "Alperose", in 1985, voted the biggest Swiss hit of all time. The song is about a romantic night spent on the Blüemlisalp in the Bernese Oberland. The popular Alperose is, in fact, a rhododendron, one of the two native species. The *Rhododendron ferrugieneum* has what look like rust marks on the leaves, and is known as the rusty-leaved Alpine Rose. The rarer *R. hirsutum* has hairy leaves, giving it the name of the hairy-leaved Alpine Rose. Both are found on mountainsides from the tree-line upwards, with glorious carmine flowers that appear from June onwards, but are not popular with farmers that raise cattle as the plants are poisonous.

Rhododendrons and their cousins, azaleas, come in all shapes and sizes, and what unites them is their preference for acidic soil. Without it, their leaves become yellow and plant fails to thrive. A few lucky areas of Switzerland have naturally occurring acidic soil, where you will find rhododendron and camellia specialists like Eisenhut in Gambarogno, Ticino (see page 129). Or visit the Camellia Park, over the lake in Locarno (see page 125). Everyone else has to make do with special acidic beds, growing in containers, or a mixture of the two. Rhododendrons come in lots of different shapes and sizes, as well as flower colours, from the tiny R. "Ptarmigan" at 50cm tall to the huge *R. giganteum* which can reach 30m tall, so you're sure to find one that's right for your garden.

The biggest rhododendron garden in Switzerland is the Seleger Moor (page 111) which is situated on top of an old peat bog, providing naturally acidic soil, perfect for raising rhododendrons, azaleas, camellias and more. It's a good example, too, of how to create an ideal rhododendron garden. Robert Seleger started by planting a shelter belt, to screen his precious plants from the cold winds that blow over this region. Rhododendrons do grow in very inhospitable conditions, but when it's very cold, they prefer to huddle under blankets of snow, protected from ice and cold, drying winds. If you can create similar conditions in your garden, with acidic soil and protection from cold winds, then you're halfway to creating a rhododendron paradise like the Seleger Moor.

RESOURCES

Garden Centres

The best garden centres have a wide range of plants, expert staff that can advise you on the best plants for your garden, and can order a special plant for you if needed as well. Many also host shows of orchids or butterflies, as well as running regular courses or advice sessions. Here are some of my favourites

- *Schwitter* are well known for their superb collection of rhododendrons and azaleas, as well as their specimen trees and Mediterranean plants.
  Gärtnerei Schwitter AG, Herzighaus, 6034 Inwil
- *Daepp*, like all of the garden centres on the list, are an old family firm, and have recently added a new concept, an "experience nursery" (see garden 20). The staff are helpful and knowledgeable, and the plants are impeccable. Worth a detour to find that special plant, or just to stock up on perennials and annuals.
  Bärenstutz 7, 3110 Münsingen, Switzerland
- *Schilliger* is a by-word for plant quality, for garden-lovers in Suisse Romande. They produce the majority of their plants themselves at their nursery in Gland, and the plants are well-adapted to the local climate.
  Route Suisse 40, 1196 Gland, Switzerland, also stores in Plan-les-Ouates and Matran (Canton Fribourg)
- *Wyss* have 6 stores, including an urban gardening store for city-dwellers in Bern, as well as an enviably busy program of courses on a huge range of topics. Their oldest store is at Zuchwil (see garden number 27) with an attractive park and a large trials area where they test seed varieties.
  Schachenweg 14, 4528 Zuchwil, Switzerland, plus 5 other stores in Ostermundigen, Oberwil, Muttenz, Bern and Aarau.
- *Garten-Center Meier AG* only have one store, but what a store it is! They have a huge selection of vegetable, fruit, herbs and equipment for urban and balcony gardening, as well as lots of great quality perennials, shrubs and even trees. You'll find a good show garden here as well, if you need ideas about what plants to mix together, and the staff are super-friendly and very well trained. They can help diagnose plant pest and disease problems and suggest the best ways to treat them, as well as running courses throughout the year. The café/restaurant is very popular with locals just popping in for coffee!
  Kreuzstrasse 2, 8635 Dürnten, Switzerland

Specialists

When you're looking for something really special, then a plant specialist is the best solution.

Roses

- *Alain and Gisèle Tschanz*, heritage, botanical and modern roses, check website for details
  Route de Bussigny 1, 1123 Aclens, Switzerland
- *Huber Roses*, breeders of roses and a large nursery and show garden (see also Garden 33 in Kanton Aargau)
  Rotenbühlstrasse 8, 5605 Dottikon, Switzerland

Rhododendrons

- *Schwitter and Daepp* (see above for details) have an excellent selection. The *Seleger Moor* nursery (see garden 44) is outstanding, open from spring to autumn, perfect for choosing your plant in bloom.
  Seleger-Moor-Strasse, 8911 Rifferswil, Switzerland
- *Vivaio Eisenhut* (see garden 52) have an extensive collection of rhododendrons, azaleas and camellias, as well as citrus, day-lilies and more. Check website for opening hours.
  Via Parco Botanico 21, San Nazarro

Conifers

- *Meylan* in Renens have a huge selection and produce an enormous number of their plants themselves. They can advise and suggest the best conifer, and any other tree or shrub, for your garden.
  Pépinières MEYLAN & Cie, Chemin de Pallettes 10, 1020 Renens

- *Anderegg* have a superb collection of conifers, as well as cloud-pruned specimens, and on-site and in-nursery advice too.
Anderegg Baumschulen AG Lotzwilfeldweg 24A, CH-4900 Langenthal
- *Ingold* have a broad range of conifers, as well as many other trees, shrubs, and ready-grown hedges. Visit the nursery or order on line.
Ingold Baumschulen AG, Weissenried, 4922 Bützberg

Fruit and vegetables
- Most garden centres have a reasonable range, perfect for beginners, but if you want something a bit more unusual, then try *ProSpecieRara* (see page 76 and 77). They host several local markets at various locations and have stalls at many spring plant fairs where you can buy both seeds and seedling plants. For "top fruit" (apples, pears etc.) *Daepp* have an enormous range, and lots of good local knowledge, as do the wonderful *Europlant* in Vich.
Route de l'Etraz 14, 1267 Vich, Switzerland

Outdoor orchids
- Outdoor, fully hardy orchids, are increasing in popularity, and many garden centres now stock a limited selection, mostly produced under the name "Garden Orchid." Johann Blättler grows and sells a broad selection.
Gartenorchideen Johann Blättler, Chatzenrain 18, CH-6064 Kerns
- You'll find some additional plants for sale at one of the regular orchid shows at the garden centres or hosted by the Swiss Orchid Society.

Perennials
Great nurseries for perennials abound in Switzerland, as well as some sumptuous gardens devoted to these lovely plants (see Gardens 5, 15, 25, 30, 32, 40, 46).
- Xavier Allemann's garden and nursery *lautrejardin* (see Garden 15) is a must-visit if you are in the region, and the nursery and catalogue are extensive. Xavier works with two other perennials nurseries, the Pépinière Biolley in Polliez-Pittet, and Rémy Jäggi's nursery and shop in

Trélex. Between them they can rapidly supply large or very varied orders, just check the catalogue and get in touch.
- There are also dozens of other nurseries like *Vogt* (Vogt Staudengärtnerei, Wannenstrasse 21, 8703, Erlenbach) or Labhart (Alte Seonestrasse 26, 5503 Schafisheim) who sell on line as well as at their nursery. Check the list of partners on the Swiss Perennials Society (Gesellschaft Schweizer Staudenfreunde or the Amis Suisses des Plantes Vivaces) for suggestions.

Alpines
- All the garden centres listed above, particularly *Schwitter*, and also the Fribourgeois garden centre *Aebi-Kaderli* (Stockera 1, 3186 Düdingen) have a good selection. *Patricia Willi* runs a perennials nursery concentrating on indigenous plants, including alpines, as well as water plants, grasses and seed mixes.
Die Wildstaudengärtnerei, Neumühle 2, Waldibrücke, 6274 Eschenbach

Pelargoniums
- The *Geranium Market* in Bern is a great source of both traditional and new varieties, but if you can't get there, then most garden centres have a good selection from May to early July. *Schilliger* (see above) have more heritage and fragrant varieties, and *ProSpecieRara* always have some interesting plants in their catalogue as well as at their markets.

Wild daffodils
- Not too far from one of the gardens described in this book (Garden 5, Le Diable Vert), you'll find one of the many wonders of Swiss flora, the wild daffodils of the Swiss Riviera. As soon as the snow melts, in April and May, the slopes above Vevey and Montreux are covered in these white, fragrant daffodils. The Chemin des Narcisses from the village of Avant will take you through some of the best meadows, as well as walks from the stations of Les Pléïades and Mont-Pèlerin, among others. Make a daytrip of it and see the garden and the daffodils!

PHOTOGRAPHY CREDITS

Where multiple photographs have been used, the photographs are referenced clockwise, from upper left.

Name of garden	Page	Photographer(s) copyright
Introduction	6	Hester Macdonald
Conservatoire et Jardin Botanique Genève	8	Conservatoire et Jardin Botanique Genève
Jardin de la Paix	10	Thierry Parel (1, 3, 4), Hester Macdonald (2, 5, 6)
Le Jardin d'Amandolier	12	Jean-François Briguet (1), Laurence Bonvin (2), Régis Golay (3, 4)
Perennially Swiss	14	Frikarti
Arboretum du Vallon de l'Aubonne	16	Pascal Sigg
Au Diable Vert	18	Au Diable Vert
Château de Prangins	20	Odile Meylan, Hester Macdonald (2–6)
Jardin des Iris	22	Regis Colombo (1–4)
Jardin d'Exposition Baudat	24	Jean-Luc Pasquier (1–4, 6), Hester Macdonald (5)
Conifers	26	Hester Macdonald
Evologia	28	Evologia
Jardin Botanique Neuchâtel	30	Hester Macdonald
Jardin du Peyrou	32	Ville de Neuchâtel (1, 2), Hester Macdonald (3, 4)
Cottage Gardens Swiss Style	34	Emmental Tourist Board
Jardin Botanique Fribourg	36	Jardin Botanique Fribourg (1, 3, 4), Hester Macdonald (2)
Château de Gruyères	38	Château de Gruyères (1, 3, 4), Hester Macdonald (2)
Roseraie d'Estavayer-le-lac	40	Hester Macdonald
lautrejardin	42	Jean-Luc Pasquier (1, 3), Hester Macdonald (2, 4)
Musée de l'Art et Histoire	44	Jean-Luc Pasquier
Papiliorama	46	Papiliorama
A Land of Roses	48	Hester Macdonald
Alpengarten Schynige Platte	50	Alpengarten Schynige Platte
Botanischer Garten der Universität Bern	52	Adrian Moser (1), Markus Bürki (2–6)
Gartenpflanzen Daepp	54	Gartenpflanzen Daepp (1, 2, 4, 5), Jean-Luc Pasquier (3, 6)
Elfenau Park	56	Christian Flück, Liebefeld (1, 6), Hester Macdonald (2, 3, 4, 5)
Oeschberg Gartenbauschule	58	Jean-Luc Pasquier (1, 2), Hester Macdonald (3–6)
Bern Rosengarten	60	Marcus Schibig (1, 2, 4), Hester Macdonald (3)

Schloss Bümpliz	62	Hester Macdonald (1–6)
Staudengarten Schulz	64	Staudengarten Schulz
Tropenhaus	66	Tropenhaus
Alpine gardens	68	Alpengarten Schynige Platte
Garten Haus Wyss	70	Wyss (1, 2, 5), Hester Macdonald (3, 4, 6)
Botanischer Garten der Universität Basel	72	Hester Macdonald (1–6)
Fondation Beyeler	74	Mark Niedermann (1, 4), Mathias Mangold (2), Hester Macdonald (3),
Wenkenpark	76	Hester Macdonald (1–6)
ProSpecieRara	78	Hester Macdonald
Ermitage Arlesheim	80	Ermitage Arlesheim
Merian Gärten	82	Christoph Merian Stiftung, Kathrin Schulthess (1, 2, 4, 5, 6), Christoph Merian Garten, A Baumeyer (3)
Swiss orchids	84	Anthura
Huber Rosen und Pflanzencenter	86	Huber Rosen
Luzerner Garten	88	Luzerner Garten (1, 2, 3), Hester Macdonald (4)
Schloss Heidegg	90	Schloss Heidegg
Geraniums	92	Hester Macdonald
Alter Botanischer Garten	94	Hester Macdonald (1–4)
Belvoir Park	96	Grün Stadt Zürich (1, 3, 4), Giorgio de Arb (2)
Botanischer Garten Zürich	98	Hester Macdonald (1–6)
Chinagarten	100	Hester Macdonald (1, 2), Grün Stadt Zürich (3, 4)
FIFA Garden	102	Bert Stankowski (1–4)
Klus Park	104	Hester Macdonald (1–6)
MFO Park	106	Raderschall (1–4)
Palais Rechberg	108	Hager Partner (1–6)
Seleger Moor	110	Seleger Moor (1–3)
Sukkulenten Sammlung	112	Urs Eggli (1), Michael Lio (2, 5), Priska Gisi (3, 4), Arto Donikyan (6)
ZHAW Wädenswil	114	Erich Stütz (1–6)
Urban Gardening	116	Urban Agriculture Basel
Baummuseum Enea	118	Hester Macdonald (1–6)
Isole di Brissago	120	Ticino Turismo, Enrico Pescantini (1), Hester Macdonald (2–6)
Parco San Grato	122	Andrea Badrutt (1), Switzerland Tourism – Roland Gerth (2), Ticino Turismo – Remy Steinegger (3), Hester Macdonald (4)
Parco delle Camelie	124	Ascona-Locarno Tourism – Alessio Pizzicanella (1–4)
Parco Scherrer	126	Ticino Turismo – Milo Carpi
Vivaio Eisenhut e Parco Botanico Gambarogno	128	Eisenhut
Rhododendrons	130	Hester Macdonald

CPSIA information can be obtained
at www.ICGtesting.com
Printed in the USA
BVHW020042270319
543613BV00065B/2799/P